Getting Over It! is an easy-to-read book that shows you how to bring your best self to the challenging, often painful experience of divorce. With the authority of someone who's "been there," Len Stauffenger explores important themes such as courage, forgiveness, how to be present with your children, taking personal responsibility, communication, and honesty – all of which will translate into greater success and satisfaction in all your relationships.

~ Jennifer Read Hawthorne, co-author *Chicken Soup for the Woman's Soul* and *Life Lessons for Loving the Way You Live*, www.jenniferhawthorne.com

Life's profound and eternal truths shine through this roadside guide. It will help everyone navigate the relationship curves and detours more thoughtfully. Loss is tough. Parenting can be difficult at times. Len's been there – done that – and successfully walked the road. So get comfy, take his hand, read this book, and you will envision yourself a more successful traveler through life's bumps.

~ Foster W. Cline, M.D., www.loveandlogic.com

Full of practical advice not only for single parents, but for ALL parents! I wish I had this book years ago for all my struggling divorced friends. You owe it to yourself and those you love to share this book!

~ GiGi Konwin, Self-Help Product Reviews

❦

This is a very practical book that will help divorced parents gain perspective and move with some measure of health toward parenting, in spite of the never-ending crisis of divorce. In fact, this book will help anyone who is open to growth and maturity.

> *~ Bishop F. Josephus Johnson, II, Presiding Bishop of the Beth-El Fellowship of Visionary Churches, Senior Pastor of The House of the Lord, Author of God is Greater Than Family Mess and The Eight Ministries of the Holy Spirit*

In Getting Over It!, Len Stauffenger offers practical advice to those dealing with the challenging tasks of raising kids after a divorce. I believe this book serves as a valuable guide to those interested in the wellbeing of their children.

> *~ Rev. Father Alberto R. Cutié, President and General Director, Pax Catholic Communications, www.paxcc.org*

Consider this great little book as a wonderful gift to yourself and anyone you know who is dealing with divorce. It's a quick read, packed with powerful options for altering perspective during a difficult time. Len has reduced this experience to manageable moments that will impact your family's future when reframed with his valuable assistance.

> *~ Judy Winslow, Coach/Consultant, www.judywinslow.com*

❦

GETTING OVER IT!
Wisdom For Divorced Parents

Len Stauffenger

MacKenzie Publishing
Akron, Ohio

MacKenzie Publishing, LLC
460 White Pond Dr.
Akron, Ohio, 44320.
www.WisdomForDivorcedParents.com
www.gettingoveritthebook.com

Library of Congress Cataloging-in-Publication Data

Stauffenger, Len.

  Getting over it! : wisdom for divorced parents / by
 Len Stauffenger.

  p. cm.

  Includes bibliographical references.

  ISBN-13: 978-0-9796836-0-2

  ISBN-10: 0-9796836-0-2

  1. Divorced parents. 2. Parenting. 3. Divorce--
 Psychological aspects. I. Title.

HQ759.915.S74 2009   306.89
      QBI08-600330

   Printed in the United States of America

Dedication

This book is dedicated to my parents who taught me everything I ever really needed to know, just by watching how they lived, and to my beautiful daughters, Sarah and Emily, who inspired me to be the best Dad that I could be.

Without the help of the following fantastic people, this book would not have been possible. I want to express my deep gratitude to Pat Dues and Diane Horlacher for their constant support and dedication. I owe a debt of gratitude to Mary Beth Grace for all of her hard work.

I am deeply grateful to "Sister" Pat Matson, my virtual assistant, who walked me through all of the steps I needed to take to bring this book about.

I want to thank my writing coach and editor, Marilyn Schwader, who made this book come alive.

To my soul mate, my best friend, Betsy, and her children.

A Word From the Author

Len Stauffenger was born and raised in a small town in Ohio. His parents taught him the simple wisdom of life. After ten years of marriage, he became a single parent raising two daughters, while at the same time running his own business. Life forced him to go back to simple values and to find a way to pass on to his children that simple wisdom. In this remarkable little book, he gives you, the reader, the tools to gain that same wisdom and share it with your family.

What's In It For You?

Some people will pick up this book out of nothing more than curiosity. Others will want the book out of a strong need. Still others will simply have an interest in learning about something that is important to them.

So what makes me think I can be your teacher? Well, I'm not so sure about being a teacher. I'm a little more comfortable aspiring to be a trusted adviser, a mentor. In any new business venture, my first recommendation would be to find someone who can give you advice based on his or her own experience. Likewise, I think everyone should have a mentor in real life.

In my life as a lawyer, I think of two men who fit this role. In essence, by the time I met them they had already been where I wanted to go. Both of them were very generous in sharing their experiences and knowledge with me. Ironically, they never met each other because I met them at different points in my career. Because of their generosity I became a better lawyer and the practice of law became more rewarding.

I also have two mentors in the computer industry, although they're each a couple of years younger than me.

But because I came to computers late, they know a lot more about technology than I ever will. But, again, their willingness to share their knowledge has shortened my learning curve.

Finally, I have several mentors in the book business. Interestingly, they're all women and, again, I have been able to accomplish much more than I ever thought possible because of their experience and generosity.

All of these mentors shared two common elements:

1. They had already been where I wanted to go and already knew what I wanted to know.

2. A willingness and ability to communicate what they do.

In every case I was able to learn from someone else's experience what worked and what didn't work.

What you'll get out of reading this book is knowledge and experience from someone who has already traveled the path you are on, who has faced divorce and made mistakes. A mentor who wants to share with love what I learned so that you avoid the pitfalls along the way.

Foreword

As a practicing partner with Psychological Associates of Southeastern Massachusetts, LLC, and in my work as a clinical psychologist, organizational consultant, and speaker, I have invested over 30 years trying to help individuals and organizations learn to turn crisis into opportunity. Unfortunately, in our society, divorce is a relatively common occurrence, and often a crisis for couples and their children. As a partner in a large clinical practice, I have had the privilege of meeting couples and individuals in all stages of the divorce process. I have also worked with children and adolescents impacted by divorce. It is a very difficult time for all involved. Also, it can be a very lonely and scary time – nobody is ever quite sure how life will look in the future. Parents worry about their children – and themselves. Children worry about their parents – and themselves!

Len's book is helpful on several fronts. First, he offers an honest and insightful description of his feelings as an individual experiencing the trauma of divorce. This includes the conflicts and concerns a loving father has for his daughters. He offers permission to feel anger, hurt, and betrayal. Yet he goes further. He offers ways to manage these feelings and ultimately provides hope that there will be another day filled with opportunity in the future. Len encourages us to step beyond the role of victim and shares the steps that helped him rebuild his life and raise his children in a loving, constructive way.

All change begins with a change in attitude. Even in a painful divorce, we will have much more success in changing our perspective, rather than changing the behavior of someone else. Len's insights about the importance of avoiding short-term battles that nobody ever wins, and instead focusing on how we envision the future, is especially important. Often the way to survive trauma in the present is to focus on what really matters most. Len helps us consider the big picture, and reminds us that children need divorcing parents to be present and to offer as much help and stability as possible.

At our practice we are adding Len's book to our "recommended" list for clients. The more that we as individuals can talk or write about our difficult experiences, the less scary the world becomes. The sense of "not traveling alone" is very reassuring.

I think you will enjoy this book and benefit from the honesty and insight that Len offers. Myself, I'm awaiting the sequel – a book by Len's daughters about life growing up with their father!

Harry Klebanoff, Ph.D.
Clinical Psychologist and Former Instructor in Psychology,
Department of Psychiatry, Harvard Medical School,
with a Psychology Degree, Yale University

A Word About the Book

This book is really about parenting and making your kids' lives better, now and in the future. Because I initially wrote it for divorced parents, the first four chapters deal with you and me: The Parents.

After writing the book, many of my friends said that every parent should read this book. It's full of little gems of wisdom. Any wisdom that's in the book, I've picked up along the way from my own experience, as well as from others.

If your divorce still affects your life, you'll probably want to read the book from the beginning. If you're just looking for the parenting wisdom, that begins at Chapter 5, although I think the first four chapters are interesting, too.

Contents

GETTING OVER IT

Chapter 1

My Story

"When one door of happiness closes, another opens; but often we look so long at the closed door that we do not see the one which has been opened for us."
~ Helen Keller

About fifteen years ago, my little family hit a bump in the road. A big bump. You could say one of the wheels fell off. Without warning, my wife wanted out of our marriage.

That period of time was precarious for my children and me. I was soon to become a single dad raising two young girls on my own. Our world had been turned upside down, and the future looked pretty scary.

Fortunately, the system I began to use from what I learned during those long, dark days in the beginning

worked out great for my kids and me. Now, I want to tell you how it can work for you, too.

Raising my daughters was the most important job I'll ever have. They are now young adults and my job is more that of a consultant. I've got everything I need. My kids are happy and healthy, and they are everything I had hoped for. I have enough money and things. So what's next in my life?

Did you ever do anything good for someone else? It makes you feel good, doesn't it? Well, that's why I'm writing this book. This story of how I became free has been in my head for ten years or more because I knew I had a formula that worked. It will help you and your children, even though I don't know you. My hope is that you learn what I learned, only much faster.

Looking back, I can see that I made some good choices. I made mistakes, but I also did some things right. Although raising my children was the hardest job I'll ever have, it was also the most rewarding. It was all worth it many times over. I want to share with you what worked. So here is my story.

The Initial Shock

This is the story of how I became free. It was the summer of 1992, and I was planning to take my wife out to the nicest restaurant in town to celebrate our tenth anniversary. We had two beautiful daughters, who at the time were about six and eight years old. It was one of those hot, summer days when life feels hectic and stressful. We had no air conditioning – just a bunch of crazy little kids running through the house.

But I've always been an optimist, and I think a day filled with laughing kids is normal. I was thinking about making dinner reservations at the expensive restaurant that I really couldn't afford, when my wife said, "Sit down. We have to talk."

I could see from the look on her face that this was something serious. She looked me in the eye and asked, "Are you happy?"

No one ever accused me of being a genius, but I knew this wasn't good. I told her, "I'd like to be a millionaire and have my own harem; but all things considered, this is about what I expect out of life at this stage of the game."

Then it got more stressful. She said, "I'm not happy."

To be honest, I wasn't really surprised. I knew she wasn't happy. I knew she hadn't been happy. I just didn't know for how long. I asked her if she wanted a divorce and she said, "Absolutely not. You're the only person in the whole world who has ever loved me, including my parents."

Now, I'm going to shorten the story up for you because for the next six months or so she continued to be not happy, but did not want a divorce. There was never an explanation about what she was not happy about. However, when I would press her, she would only say, "You're a good husband and a great father. I'm just not happy."

The problem was, there was never anything I could fix. Nothing like, "You drink too much," or "You play too much golf." That was hard for me because I'm a fixer. I was brought up that way. Identify the problem and then go after it and solve it. But, in this case, there was no way to identify the problem. There was nothing to fix. How you do make someone happy?

Looking For A Pattern

In hindsight, I don't think she was ever happy. I missed seeing that because I met her in college, and let's face it, in college there are no jobs, no dirty diapers, no bills to pay; in short, there's no stress beyond getting good grades.

Her unhappiness was not a surprise because for years she hadn't been happy. But her unhappiness had always been focused on other people – she didn't have any friends, or she hated her friends, or she was mad at her parents, or she hated her sister, or she hated her part-time job, etc. I was always the one good thing in her life.

But I'm not completely stupid, and eventually I saw the pattern. In short, nothing ever met her expectations, and I started to wonder when I would be in that category, too. I suppose I should have seen it coming. I suppose I did see it coming, but denied it. It's awfully hard to admit to painful issues when you have two little kids who might be affected. My approach was to always make it better. Just keep beating your head against the wall, and one day you'll knock the wall down.

Change of Plans

For those six months, life was hell. She didn't want a divorce, but she wasn't happy. Eventually, I realized that I really wouldn't mind being free from her. In fact, I eventually saw how great that would be! But I was terrified for my children. What would happen to my little girls? At six and eight years old, you're pretty damn vulnerable. What harm might come to them if we split up?

By this time, in my mind, it was about *when* we split not *if*, and my imagination was running wild. What if she remarries and tries to take them to another state and I only see them twice a year? I didn't think I could survive that. Or worse, what would it do to them? I was a very hands-on dad. When I came home from work, I took over. I played games with them, read them bedtime stories, and tucked them in every night.

Finally, after six months of unhappiness, she said she wanted a divorce. She never did really give me a valid reason. She just stood in our kitchen and screamed at me, "I want out of this marriage now!"

So there you have it. I was 33 years old. I was the father of two beautiful, healthy kids. I owned a house in the suburbs, and was looking forward to a bright future. Ooops! Change of plans. Hey, if somebody wants out, they're out! What could I do?

I accepted her decision. I told her she could have all of our things, but I wanted the kids. I had one goal at this point – to raise my two daughters so they would be happy and healthy. I knew that what we decided at that point would have an impact on my girls their entire lives. A pretty heavy thought.

Feeling Like a Failure

Before I finish that part of our divorce story, I want to give you a little side note so you know I understand what you're going through. For many months, maybe even a year or two after our divorce, I felt empty. I felt like a complete failure. My parents have been married for over 50 years and theirs is a happy marriage. They really do like, as well as love, each other. I have two brothers who are both happily married to terrific women. In a sense, you could say their marriages mirror my parent's union – they like and love each other and have happy home lives. I also have relatives who are happily married.

Some of the people in my family refer to me as "The Smart One" because I was the first member of the family to go to college. So here I was, "The Smart One," a complete and utter failure at the most important job of my life. At least, that's the way I thought about myself at the time.

At the age of 33, I gave my wife my house and everything in it and I moved into a small, two-bedroom apartment. I bought some cheap furniture; I was driving a leased Pontiac Grand-Am; I had no bank accounts or assets. I had $18,000 in debt (credit card bills of $8,000 and my student loan of $10,000). And yet, I was full of joy, because I no longer had to live with an unhappy person, and I knew the kids were going to be in my life.

Setting Us Free

We got our divorce and agreed that the kids would live with each of us a month at a time, alternating back and forth between her house and my apartment. That agreement lasted for about a year, when the girls said they wanted to live with me all summer and just go back and forth during the school year. My ex didn't like that, but she went along with it.

The next year, the girls said they wanted to live with Dad all spring and all summer and that they'd go back and forth in the winter. The ex really didn't like that.

We never went to court and battled over it, but she put a lot of pressure on the kids and told them she would disown them. That's a terrible thing to say to your ten-year-old.

I'm not going to tell you my ex and I are friends. We're not. I'm grateful to her for having given me two wonderful children who will be a part of me for eternity. I hold no animosity toward her, any hatred or anger. I just set her free. And that set me free. I believe it also set our daughters free. Freedom is the starting point.

GETTING OVER IT

Chapter 2

Get Your Head Right

"I know God will not give me anything I can't handle.
I just wish that He didn't trust me so much."
~ *Mother Theresa*

Giving my ex what she asked for gave us all a new beginning. But it was just a start; I had a lot to learn about being an effective parent.

The first thing I realized was that my daughters needed stability, a place to feel safe. Divorcing had set us all free, and at the same time, my children also needed stability. There's always a balance.

I saw very quickly that the first step in being an effective parent is to get your head right. You've got to put yourself in a place where you're free from the pain of divorce, and free from a connection to the ex. I hope you notice all the "you's" and "your's" in that sentence, because this next chapter is about you and getting free from your story, as I did mine.

Be Fully Present With Your Kids

I remember very clearly driving to a family birthday party with the kids shortly after the divorce. I knew my brothers would be there with their wives and their kids and my parents – all one big, happy family. There would only be one failure in the family – me.

I know I drove there with the kids, but I can't tell you if we had any conversation, because I wasn't there. My mind was focused on feeling sorry for myself. As we were driving to this big family gathering, I was focused on how our family had been split up, and wondering about what harm would come to my children.

In actuality, the kids had already dealt with the divorce. Let's face it, what choice do kids have? Mom and Dad are split up! Usually, the fear of what they are experiencing is worse than the reality. They realize that Mom and Dad still love them and that Mom and Dad are still a part of their life. It may not be what they chose, but they accept it. If anything, they're wondering what happens next.

To be a truly effective parent, you have to be with your kids mentally, physically, spiritually, and emotionally. Just because you're having dinner with them, and you're physically with them, if your mind is on work, you are not really there. Likewise, if your mind is on the pain of your divorce or your anger at your ex, you're not really there for your kids – you're not with them. And if you're not there mentally and emotionally, they know it. They feel the loss of you. They may not know what you're thinking about (which is probably a good thing), but they know you're not there with them.

Every time you're with your children, you have an opportunity to be a positive influence on them, and you both miss out if you are mentally somewhere else.

Maybe you're consumed with this feeling of anger or disappointment – disappointment in yourself, disappointment in your ex, fear, feelings of failure, lonelines, etc. You're concerned about how this affects them, and yet you're making it worse because you're not fully present.

Be You!

So how do you set yourself free and become present for your children? Be you!

The best thing that can happen is for Dad to just be Dad. Talk to your children, interact with them, have fun with them, teach them.

Instead of being present and with my daughters on the ride to the family gathering, I wasted that opportunity and spent the time living in my head.

The good news is that I got past my immature, self-absorption very quickly, and you can, too. It's a process and there are steps you have to go through. I'm going to take you through those steps and in doing so, you can get through that process more quickly.

Acceptance: Be With It

So what do I mean when I say, "Be with it"? Another way of saying it is, "Accept it." Accept the end of the marriage in all its gory details. Embrace the pain. That may sound strange to you, but it's important, so let's talk about it for a little bit.

The First Step in Acceptance is Courage

The first step in acceptance is courage – the courage to let your guard down and accept all the fears that are rumbling around in your head. They're already there; acknowledgé them. How will it look to my family? How will it look to my friends? Will the people I work with talk about me behind my back?

He or she betrayed you. The marriage failed. Whatever you're afraid of, it's already happened, or it never will. You have no control over it. Whether your parents are angry or feel sorry for you, or however they feel, they've already felt it. Whatever your fears are about your friends and co-workers are probably exaggerated in your mind, but whatever those fears are – that they are laughing at you, or they pity you, or whatever – they've already done it or they never will.

We think we're more important to other people than we really are. Maybe they'll make a brief comment about your situation. Maybe they'll even talk about it once or twice over lunch. I promise you that they don't talk about you nearly as much as you think they do. They have their own problems. People are focused on their own little worlds, their husbands, wives, lovers, children, money.

If you can't get past this, then let yourself imagine they are talking about you. Conjure up all the nastiness you think they might say. Whatever your fears are, face them. Everyone worries about looking good or, alternatively, not looking bad. Everybody. If you want to impress someone, go through a difficult time with dignity. Show true strength. Most people don't have it in them.

Courage is Rewarded

When you face your fears, they shrink. When you resist them, they grow. For examples of this, you need look no further than your children and other people in your life. At times, your son or daughter was afraid or worried or nervous about something or someone. Maybe it was as simple as standing up in front of people at the spelling bee at school. Maybe it was a friend or relative who had to deal with something they didn't want to deal with. As an outsider, you could observe their situation and you knew they were causing themselves more pain than was necessary.

My dad used to say, "Everyone takes their turn in the barrel." Now it's your turn. Be an outsider and look at your situation objectively. Know that if you have courage and face your fears, they'll shrink away to nothing.

If you still have trouble doing this for yourself, then do it for your children. Be brave for them. You have the courage to stand in front of a bullet for them, so you certainly have the courage to face your fears. You need to become emotionally healthy so that they can be healthy.

Embrace The Pain

You may feel like a real victim and feel like the only person who has ever gone through the painful feeling divorce stirs up. You're not. No one gets married and has kids with the intention of getting a divorce, and yet statistics say that 35% of first marriages end in divorce. The 50% figure you often hear about in pop culture is a combination of first and second marriages, because the rate for second marriages ending in divorce is higher than first marriages. So understand, you are not alone in facing pain caused by a divorce!

Let's acknowledge that you are in pain now, and here I am telling you to embrace the pain as a second step. You probably think I'm nuts and you're asking yourself, "Is he a masochist?" The answer is, "No." I want to show you how to go beyond the pain.

Ultimately, to break through the pain and come out pain-free on the other side, it's important to learn to just be with it, or simply accept the pain. This is what ultimately allows you to let the relationship go. This isn't anything new. Keep in mind this is not some "New Age" advice. This is wisdom from ancient times. Folks have been going through these emotions and feelings for a millennium. The problem is that we human beings don't like pain, so we resist it. By resisting it, we make it more intense and we make it last longer.

Not only do we resist pain, we often refuse to look at it. The longer we refuse to deal with it, the longer we suffer. An old Reiki master once summed it up for me this way: "On the other side of pain is joy."

This will work for any relationship. You are now in charge of your future. The first step is up to you.

A Note To You, the Reader: Be Objective About Your Own Situation

To really get what I mean about embracing the pain, I want to offer a piece of advice on how to view the situation you are in: Think in terms of someone else. It's very hard for us to be objective about our own situation. As an example, imagine you were counseling someone else. It can be anyone, a friend or a relative, but make it someone real and then give him or her your problem. As much as possible, take an objective viewpoint. If that's too difficult, find someone else that will play that role for you. Then think about what I'm about to lay out for you.

Get Over It!

It's really pretty simple isn't it? You've tried, she's tried, but it's over. You might say, "Well, [he or she] didn't try. [He or She] just gave up too easily." You may be right. In fact, you are most likely correct.

But think about it if you were counseling someone else, say a friend whose husband wanted a divorce – and your friend was absolutely right. She had been a wonderful mother, she had always been loyal, and in return her husband had cheated on her with someone at work and now wanted to abandon her and the children, and you knew, as her friend, that it was over. You truly care about her and you hope and wish that she could somehow get past the emotion. Because, even though she's right and he's wrong, you know that it doesn't matter. She can bring in witnesses, friends, and relatives to prove that she is right and he is wrong. But it doesn't matter.

And still your friend yells out, "We were married for ten years, we have children; this is so wrong; he's a bastard!"

It doesn't matter. It's over. Done is done. Live in the present, not the past. Get over it.

But how do you actually do that? We're getting to the point where we start to understand what it means to truly Be With It.

There is Usually Someone Else

I'm going to give you a concrete example of how to Be With It, an example that will help you whatever your circumstances.

When I was going through my divorce, a friend told me, "There's always someone else." Instinctively, I believed it to be true; emotionally, I didn't want to accept it. How could that be true if I was so wonderful?

In many cases there is someone else, and in some cases, you might even know who that someone else is. In other cases, you believe it's true, but you're not sure who it is. Some of you may continue to resist the idea that there is someone else. And a very few of you might actually be right, that there is no one else. Regardless of the truth of someone else being in your ex's life, facing the reality that you are not "The One" anymore and that someone is or will be in your place, is critical in getting over it.

We live in a politically correct world. The problem is that people seldom say what they really mean. I'm not politically correct. I have on more than one occasion been accused of being a black-and-white kind of guy. The problem with political correctness and dancing around subjects is that it is not honest, nor is it accurate. When people are going through a divorce, their friends and their family say things like, "He's seeing someone," or "She has a boyfriend," or "We think there's someone else." The response in my mind is, "You bet your ass he's seeing someone. He's seeing every inch of her."

Be brutally honest with yourself. You're not worried about him "seeing" someone; you're worried about him sleeping with someone. You're not upset that she's interested in someone else. You're upset that she's with another man.

I'm not interested in being crude here, nor am I trying to write some kind of erotic novel. This is what I meant above when I said, "Embrace the pain in all its gory details." The more honestly you tell yourself the truth, the more graphic you are with the details, the more you fully appreciate the betrayal, the better off you'll be. Because when you can be with it, you get to the joy on the other side.

Removing the Band-Aid

It's human nature not to like to deal with unpleasant things, unpleasant situations, or unpleasant people. It's also human nature to suffer. But smart humans get past the suffering by dealing with their demons straight up.

When I was a kid, anyone who got sick was dragged to the doctor's office for a shot. We would always moan and cry and whine about not wanting to go. We would make every argument we could think of, and ultimately our mom would drag us kicking and screaming to the doctor's for a shot. Every time, it made us feel better, but damn, that shot hurt! Even though we were kids, we knew the shot made us feel better. But we still didn't want to go the next time. Even though the pain of the shot was intense and was very brief, the fear of that pain made us choose to stay home and be sick. Fortunately, we didn't get to make that choice. Mom just dragged us to the doctor's and that was the right choice.

The lesson here is: Deal with the quick, intense pain, and get over that long, dragged-out, torturous stuff. You can peel the Band-Aid off slowly and painfully, or you can pull it off quickly and be done with it. Your choice.

You've got kids, and because you have kids, you know what I'm saying is true. You can think up examples in your own life where your kids resisted something unpleasant or painful and you just knew they would be better off in the long run if they would deal with it now.

That's where we're all just big kids.

Try To Make It Worse!

So face your fears; dredge up whatever is the most painful thing for you. It may be that for you the most painful thing is to think of your husband with that other woman at the nicest restaurant in town laughing, joking, touching, gazing into each other's eyes, having a wonderful time while you are at home making dinner for the kids. You might not even know if that example actually happened. Just imagine that it did, and then make it worse.

Maybe for you it's the thought of your wife having sex with another man. Don't push that thought away. Think about it, dwell on it, and make it worse. Whatever bothers you the most, imagine they did it. I can't tell you exactly what you should think of. You know what it is. It's whatever hurts you the most, whatever it is that you're afraid of the most. Imagine that it is happening, and I promise you that once you come to grips with that reality, once you accept it, it will be less painful than constantly trying to push that thought out of your head.

Resistance Is Futile

Your resistance keeps you from engaging with your children. It's your resistance to what is so that's causing you pain, even though you want to blame the ex for making you feel that pain. That resistance is what's cheating you out of your life and out of spending time with your children. It's also cheating your children.

You Can Only Control Your Reaction

He doesn't love you anymore. She loves someone else. You may wonder why, and you may want answers. I would encourage you to get answers and we'll talk more about that later. But for now, accept that they no longer want to be with you. If you need to, imagine that she's had affairs with other people. It may help you to imagine that he's never been faithful to you or that he ever loved you. It doesn't matter. Done is done. You've heard this before: You can't control what other people do; you can only control how you react to it.

This isn't just for those of you whose spouses left for conventional affairs. The same exercise applies if your wife left you for another woman or if your husband left you for another man. Maybe they just left because they're tired of you, or because they wanted to go find themselves. It all comes down to the same thing: They don't want to be with you anymore. You have absolutely no control over that; you can't change it. You never will. The good news is that you have absolute control over how you react to it and how you deal with it.

You're absolutely right: He's a jerk; she's a tramp. Life is not fair. You have brown eyes and you wanted blue. You're short and you wanted to be tall. You trusted someone, and they betrayed you. But done is done. It could be the greatest learning experience of your life. It could open up doors to joy and pleasure that you never dreamed of. And no matter what he did to you or how she betrayed you, they're not doing it to you now. You're doing it to yourself! Even if you can't accept how tall or short you are or whether you like the color of your eyes, it's all a done deal. Refusing to accept it is the source of your pain.

Chapter 2 - Things to Consider

❖ There's a balance between freedom and stability.

❖ The steps to freedom.

❖ Be present.

❖ Face your fears and they will shrink; when you resist them they grow.

❖ On the other side of pain is joy.

❖ Refusing to accept causes the pain.

Getting Over It

Chapter 3

Forgive Yourself

"Our children are not going to be just our children – they are going to be other people's husbands and wives and the parents of our grandchildren."
~ Mary Steichen Calderone

Forgiving yourself should be a lot easier than forgiving your ex. After all, they're the one who caused all the problems. But just so we don't leave any loose ends, you should at least explore what your role was.

Your Role In All This

I think of the process of forgiveness of self in three steps. The first is to decide what your role was in the marriage failing. Next is to accept responsibility in some way. Then forgive yourself and move forward.

I had a client who, for many years had been in business with a partner. They had done very well. They had made money and had fun doing it. But over time they became suspicious of each other. They each began to protect their own turf. They each began to view the other in a different light. Suddenly, each of them knew he was right and his partner was wrong. They ended up suing each other, spending tens of thousands of dollars and almost two years entangled in a mess.

My client, who was a good man, literally despised his former partner and blamed everything on him. The attorney representing the partner told me his client saw things exactly the same way but from his side. His client believed that he was entirely in the right and that my client had somehow become evil.

The point is, that both the other attorney and I could see that neither of these men was evil. We could objectively look at the situation as outsiders and see how miscommunication and misperception had caused the two of them to spiral out of control. If they could have seen their role in the downward spiral and what brought about the downfall of their business without assigning blame, they could have transformed a very bad situation into something very positive. Instead, the business was destroyed. And they both walked away bitter, certain that it was all the other guy's fault.

Good Reasons or Excuses?

Just for a moment, pretend it doesn't matter who's at fault. Just ask yourself how it is you chose to have children with this person? Now immediately, your mind may come up with some reasons (sometimes called excuses) such as "I was young, I was dumb, I was fooled, he tricked me, she lied, they weren't who they pretended to be, etc." Don't you want to know how it is you were fooled?

At your wedding, you swore the most solemn oath you will ever swear in your life – that you would spend the rest of your life with this person. You made a complete and total commitment. You made an implied promise to your future children that it would last forever. So let's face it, unless you figure out your role, it could happen again. Do you remember that I mentioned earlier the divorce rate is much higher for second marriages?

Owning Your Part vs. Blame

Acknowledging and owning your part in the failure of the marriage all comes down to courage. It comes down to being responsible only for you. I've met many divorced people, and usually the ones who are more interested in finding answers seem to be the ones who were less at fault. I'm not saying that sarcastically. I really do believe that in many situations, from an outsider's point of view, there is one who is more at fault and there is one who is less at fault. But as I've said many times, finding fault misses the point. If you wrap all your energy into pointing fingers, you won't have any left to forgive and start healing.

When I got dumped, divorced, or whatever you want to call it, I was sure that my wife was at fault. I could bring in 100 witnesses who would agree with me. Even now, years later, virtually everyone that knew each of us – even her family – would agree that she was at fault. But even back then, in the middle of the divorce, I realized very early on: It Doesn't Matter! No One Cares!

Even though all my friends, all my family, and everyone who knew us would tell you how difficult she was or how lucky I was to be away from her, it didn't matter. Even if you could have some kind of community hearing and bring in all of your friends and all of your family, and her friends or his family, and even if 100 people said you were the good one and she was the bad one, and there was an official judgment, a proclamation if you will, that you were the good guy and that she was all at fault, in fact she was a liar, a cheat, and a scoundrel, and if that judgment was printed in the local newspaper, it might make you feel a little better, but what have you accomplished? She still doesn't want you.

But most importantly, you still have children together. It certainly is not going to make your children feel any better to hear you blame their mom (or dad). If anything, it's going to be hurtful to them.

Okay, You're the Good One

On some level, you were profoundly hurt by the fact that your marriage failed. And if you're a good parent (and if you're reading this book, you are a good parent because you care), you're disappointed to your core that you've let your children down; that you've caused them pain; that you didn't create that perfect, ideal family. So, let's work on creating something really good.

Here's some reality: The perfect, ideal family is a fantasy. And on some level you know you played a role in the failure of your marriage; you bear some responsibility. You would be so wise to let go of the notion of fault, of assigning blame. That's an immature way of looking at life. Little kids point fingers and blame people.

As I said before, your husband or wife didn't get married and have children with you with the intent and design to one day wreak havoc on everyone's lives. Most people who get divorced do so because they are fundamentally incompatible. They have a different set of values.

You've probably read books and studies where they talk about the fact that the most successful marriages happen when both people have the same set of values.

Unfortunately, in life we have to make the most important decisions in our lives usually well before we have all the information. Even if your ex-husband is the most selfish S. O. B. in the state, when your children were born, he didn't want to hurt them by divorcing their mother. Even if he never acknowledges it, on some level he knows he failed his children.

If you seek out professional help on this issue, I would strongly urge you to start with the question, "What did I do that contributed to this?" You'll probably spend a little time talking about how your ex-husband is so selfish, is pathological, or how your ex-wife is a slut. Don't spend too much time on it, because they are what they are. You are better off focusing on what your part was and how you can make different choices in the future.

The Ex's Problems Are Theirs, Not Yours

Everyone knows the saying, "When life gives you lemons, make lemonade." Well, just for a moment, imagine if you really could take a bad situation and turn it into something good. What a fantastic skill! Now, imagine your children learning from you how to do that so they can use it throughout their lives.

Although everyone has the ability to acquire that skill, most people only use it occasionally. The reason is because it's easier to blame something or someone else.

They point fingers, they want to get even, and they are stuck in reverse.

The first step in transforming something bad into something good is to get over blaming, get past pointing fingers, and stop spending so much energy trying to get even. All that is just a waste of energy and has a horrible effect on your children. I'll give you an example of how this can happen.

Many years ago, the wife of a good friend of mine left him. He eventually met a woman whose husband had also left her. My friend and his girlfriend didn't know each other when their spouses left them; in fact they were living in different states. They met and fell in love. This is now a genuine loving relationship. They're just flat out happy, although they never married. After their kids grew up and went to college, the couple decided to build their dream home. They were in that dream home exactly thirteen months when his ex-wife and her third husband purchased a house on the same street. Now that's life giving you lemons.

My friends are human; they were angry, upset, and felt like their space had been invaded. They saw no way this could turn out good.

My friend's girlfriend wanted to move. My friend's reply was, "I'm not moving. I'm not going to give my ex-wife that power over me to force me out of my dream home." (Truth be told, his ex-wife wanted to cause him problems and was probably hoping he would break up with his girlfriend.) But this couple has that ability to make lemonade. How'd they do it?

As I said, at first they didn't see a way out, which caused concern for a few months. The fact is, he could have stayed in the house. He could have simply ignored his ex-wife, but the situation was upsetting his girlfriend.

She's a gentle soul who doesn't like any conflict. So he took a step back. Where initially he had drawn a line in the sand and said, "Hell no. I won't go," he now agreed that he would at least consider other options. He told me, "If I have to choose between the house and Cindy that's easy; I'd choose Cindy." In fact he told me, "Hell Len, home for me is anywhere Cindy is."

Once they let go of the anger and the upset, options started to appear. Cindy liked the idea of having a smaller house to clean. They both liked the idea of having more money in their pocket and being able to do other things that they had always wanted to do, like travel. Then they found a lot for sale with an incredible view and a house design that was smaller and even more attractive than the one they had been living in. On top of that, while building the second house, they could change the little mistakes they'd learned in building the first house.

They still had to go through all the aggravations of selling their house. Furthermore, anytime you move, it involves expenses. Plus, they had some nice neighbors they hated to leave. But as I said, this is real life not a fairy tale.

In the end, they got a house that is better suited for them, they've got more money in their pocket, and they're on a lot that's about as close to perfect as they could find. Now that's lemonade! These people have made it a habit of turning lemons into lemonade.

Their ability to make lemonade began when they let go of the anger they felt toward the ex-wife. If you ask them, sure, they'll tell you what she did was wrong, underhanded, manipulative, etc. But they can't change who she is. Their reaction was normal: They were angry and upset. My friend even told me he thought about getting even. But really, what could he do?

So the first step was to make a choice. They could stew about something they had no control over. They could whine about how life is unfair. They could blame her and her new husband (after all what kind of bozo lets his wife move in on the same street as her ex-husband?). And they could have done that with all the support of their friends and neighbors, who unanimously agreed with them. Or, they could choose to make lemonade by doing exactly what they had adamantly opposed.

I often told my children when they were growing up, "There's the way the world is, and there's the way the world ought to be. You better learn to deal with the way it is."

If your husband truly is that selfish, then he will always be that selfish. If your wife really is self-absorbed, then she'll always be. That's going to be their problem to fix. Don't let it be yours.

I would hate to go through life as the most selfish S. O. B. in the land or the biggest slut, but if that's their life sentence, well, then that falls under the category of: What goes around comes around. In my experience, the really selfish people are really unhappy people, but that's another story.

How does this relate to your children? Even children don't care who is at fault, because they have to deal with the way the world is, and that is that mom and dad don't live together anymore.

Furthermore, children have a remarkable resiliency. They can adjust to what is happening, and they can put it behind them, and they can live happy, healthy lives. How fast this happens is a direct result of how you steer the boat. If you keep showing anger toward their other parent, you continue to cause them pain and hold them back. If their dad is truly selfish, they'll see that over time on their own.

Kids learn by modeling. So keep in mind that if your ex-husband is selfish, they will be spending time around a selfish person. They need to also spend time around a healthy, happy person. That's you. They will see over time how their dad or their mom treats other people. They will see that although dad is selfish, he isn't happy. You, on the other hand, give them the example of an unselfish, caring person and they'll see that the universe brings you peace, love, and happiness.

No, your life won't be perfect. No one's is. Just remember, raising children isn't a sprint. It's a long marathon, day after day. And the best way to raise healthy, happy children is to continually strive each day to be the best person that you can be. They'll get it.

Without Blame, You Can Learn

We all see things from our own point of view and we all want to be right. In fact, we think we are right all the time. So it's almost a knee-jerk reaction that we defend our thinking when someone even hints that we are wrong. You might have even mentally defended yourself, just for a short time, while you were reading this book, or maybe just while you were reading this chapter. Don't think of things as right and wrong. Don't think in terms of blame or fault. There's a saying I like: "Do you want to be right, or do you want to get it right?"

The whole idea of taking responsibility for your role in the failure of this marriage is to gain an understanding, to learn. Nothing more. Why did you marry him? What attracted you to her? Do you remember early in the relationship being excited and in love? Do you remember a time when you thought it would last forever?

But it didn't last forever. Why not? If it was totally his fault, do you understand the consequences of that statement?

If you really believe it was totally his fault and you had nothing to do with it, then that means you are powerless in your relationship. That means, it could happen all over again and you have no say in the matter.

When you blame other people for your problems, you will always have those problems. You are really saying it is totally in their control and there is nothing you can do.

Life is ironic. People don't like to take responsibility for their actions, but when they do, it empowers them. That's the irony.

Accepting responsibility doesn't mean you're at fault. Remember, at least for this chapter, we're giving up the idea of fault. It means you have a say in the matter. It means you have some power over what happened or what is happening. Understanding that you're responsible for just about everything in your life is great. It means you get to create your life. No one else is dictating to you.

Did You See It Before the Wedding?

Let's look at a tough example. Maybe you really were a great wife and you did everything a wife should do, but your husband just never appreciated you. And you're thinking, "How was I responsible for our divorce?"

My question to you would be, "Whatever flaws your ex had, was there any sign of them before you got married? Or before you had children? Was there anything you consciously or unconsciously ignored or blinded yourself to?" Your responsibility may be nothing more than the fact that you knew he was selfish but you married him anyway.

Sometimes, very simple decisions or the failure to make a decision can cause very harsh consequences. But again, that's the way the world is. It can happen again, so aren't you better off understanding that your subtle decision to ignore his faults had a profound impact on your life? If you understand that, if you take responsibility for that piece of it, then you won't make that mistake again.

This is a lesson that applies to everything that makes you unhappy in your life, whether it's your boss, your lover or your children. Don't do what everyone else does, which is to blame the other person or the situation. Instead, the first question should be, "What's my role in this? How am I causing this or contributing to this?" Just remember, it's not about fault; it's really about consequences.

When you get this, it's a wonderful tool for your life because it allows you to solve your problems. This isn't about fault; it's about self-discovery. The more you know about yourself and the reasons for your actions and your motivation, the more satisfying and fulfilling your life becomes, because you're no longer operating on automatic pilot.

I'll give you an example from my life. When I got divorced, everyone, and I mean everyone, said I was the good guy and that she had changed during our marriage. Obviously, my ego liked hearing that. It would be tempting to sit back and say to myself, "Yes, I'm a great guy and it was all her fault and blah, blah, blah."

However, there was this lonely thought in the back of my brain saying, "Then why did you pick her?" I appreciated everyone thinking I was "right," but it was far more important for me to actually get it right. Because even if people thought I was the good guy, I was still divorced. My marriage failed. It was my life.

So I went to see a psychologist and I gave her the background and then I asked her, "I want to know what I did wrong." I'd see her every once in a while for about six months. We'd talk, explore things, and then it all came together. It all clicked.

One day she told me, "You're a strong man, so weaker women are attracted to you." By weaker she meant insecure. We all know people who are insecure and the more insecure they are, the less fun they are to be around. They tend to project their insecurities on other people.

I'm not a psychologist, but I got it. I learned something about me. I looked back and realized I dated many women who were insecure. I realized that my role in it was that on some level, my ego enjoyed the fact that they needed me.

I got it. You can't have a healthy relationship with a needy person (male or female).

Now I'm pretty sure that when I was nineteen years old, I wasn't looking for a needy woman. But my ego enjoyed all the praise and admiration she gave me, and I liked being needed. I thought she was just madly in love with me. Over time, of course, her needs didn't go away. I'm not trying to be critical of her. I just finally saw what was happening.

The exciting part for me was, I learned a huge lesson from digging deep and finding out what my role was. I grew, and as a result of my asking what my role was in the failure of my marriage, I was confident that I could find a woman that could be my equal partner.

Your Role and Forgiveness

My hope is that my example will inspire you to take responsibility in determining what your role was. Because if you figure that out, you will grow and it will carry over into all areas of your life and, even more exciting, you will be able to teach your children about true responsibility.

Remember, this chapter is about forgiving yourself. If you understand what I'm saying in this chapter so far, you understand there really isn't anything to forgive. We're all just children trying to find our way.

It's really more about understanding and acceptance. Then the forgiveness of self is easy.

So, figure out what your role was and then move forward. Don't dwell on what you could have done or what time has gone past. What's done is done.

The Daffodil Garden

There's a beautiful, true story floating around the Internet called The Daffodil Garden. In summary, a woman goes to see her daughter who insists upon taking her to see the daffodils on the side of the mountain in Running Springs, California. When the woman ultimately sees the daffodils, she is overcome because they literally cover the entire side of the mountain.

In the middle of all these glorious daffodils is a small house, where a woman named Mrs. Gene Bauer lives. Mrs. Bauer planted each one of those thousands upon thousands of daffodils. She had been planting them all by herself, since 1958.

The woman who saw these with her daughter was both inspired and a little sad because she thought of all of her lost opportunities and wondered what she could have accomplished had she moved toward her goals one step at a time. She said to her daughter, "It made me sad, in a way, to think of what I might have accomplished."

Her daughter replied, "Start tomorrow."

So start tomorrow... Stop waiting... Until your car is paid off, until you get a new car, until your kids leave the house, until you go back to school...

Until you finish school,
Until you lose 10 pounds,
Until you get married,
Until you get a divorce,
Until you have kids,

Until your kids go to school,
Until you retire,
Until summer,
Until you die.

Chapter 3 - Things to Consider

- ❖ Figure out your role.

- ❖ The steps to freedom.

- ❖ Accept "some" responsibility (i.e., learn from the past).

- ❖ Taking the long view can help you learn how to make "lemonade".

- ❖ Release yourself.

GETTING OVER IT

Chapter 4

Forgive, But Don't Forget

"Even though you may want to move forward in your life, you may have one foot on the brakes. In order to be free, we must learn how to let go. Release the hurt. Release the fear. Refuse to entertain your old pain. The energy it takes to hang onto the past is holding you back from a new life.

What is it you would let go of today?"
~ *Mary Manin Morrissey*

Honestly, I think this chapter should be titled "Forgive Him (or Her)", but I figured if I made that the name of the chapter, you'd throw the book away! But keep reading; it's worth it, and your kids need you to understand this very important piece.

You might be thinking, "This guy said his book was about raising healthy and happy kids, and we haven't even been discussing kids." You've read this far because you know that even though I haven't focused on the kids, what I'm talking about regarding acceptance and forgiveness really is about the kids. And I'll be getting to more specifics soon, so stick with me.

You can't be an effective parent until you get your own stuff together. This is the foundation. This is what allows you to be there for them today, tomorrow, and in the years to come.

This is the hardest chapter. It's even worse than imagining your husband or wife with other people. This is the one you will resist the most, so of course, it's the most important one.

Why Forgiveness?

Everyone knows forgiveness is good, right, just, and important. It's just better when someone else is doing it.

God tells you to forgive; it's in the Bible. You know about that even if you don't read the Bible. You know that every major religion in the world insists that we forgive our brothers and sisters. You know that Jesus

Christ forgave the men who whipped him and crucified him. They did a lot worse to him than your wife did to you.

Read this quote from *A Course in Miracles*, one of the most profound books I've ever read: *You who want peace can find it only by complete forgiveness.*

At your core, you know that forgiveness is the way to go. We all know instinctively that forgiveness is what God wants us to do. We also know instinctively, although sometimes it's really hard to see this, that it's best for us. But why is it so hard to forgive? Why is it that some really good people, the ones you trust your life with, can't seem to forgive someone who's done them wrong?

It's even harder to forgive if you're the one who got dumped (also known as the dumpee). My guess is that most of the people picking up this book were dumpees. I was a dumpee and some of my best friends were dumpees. In my experience over the long haul, the dumpees usually fare better. But to really do well in life, to move on with grace, they have to get past this forgiveness thing.

I really want to tell you that you have to forgive her (or him) but I won't, because it's human nature to resist when another person tells you that you have to do something. That being said, it would be really good for you and for your kids if you could forgive her (or him.)

Don't throw the book away. This is the part that's really valuable to your children. This is the part that will do the most to let your kids know everything is okay. It will help them grow up healthy and happy. You might be thinking now that you're going to throw up because I keep talking about forgiving her and all you can do is imagine her having sex with someone else, behind your back, while you were a good husband.

I'm telling you to forgive him and you think I don't understand because I'm just a stupid man and I can't possibly imagine how you feel, knowing you were taking care of little kids and making dinner and being a wonderful wife while your husband was meeting his secretary at a hotel. Let me assure you, I don't care about your cheating husband or lying wife. I care about your kids. I want to help you. This isn't about helping the person who is being forgiven. It's all about helping the one who is doing the forgiving.

Why is it so hard to forgive? Why should I forgive an injustice? And how do I forgive? How do I get to that point where I can forgive?

Understand that when you forgive your husband, you are not condoning what he did. When you forgive your wife, you are not in any way approving of what she did. Forgiveness has nothing to do with right and wrong. It has everything to do with freedom and release. Forgiveness exists for giving you the next good thing for your life.

You've probably heard the saying that revenge is like taking poison and expecting your enemy to die. It's true. As I mentioned earlier, the ancients knew these things long before we were ever born.

The truth is, no matter what your husband or wife did, you're not going to get even with them. You're certainly not going to physically harm them or kill them. You're not going to make it go away, and you're not going to make it right. They most certainly did what they did because of their own flaws and weaknesses.

Remember George, on *Seinfeld*, when he tells a women he was breaking up with, "It's not you; it's me." He was right! If your husband or wife dumped you, it really is them. That's not to say you're perfect, and I would encourage you to learn as much as you can about yourself. But if you got dumped, there was a reason for it, and most likely that reason was inside that other person. That may not make you feel any better, but they thought they had a good reason. They probably even thought they had to do it. It was more than just a desire; it was necessary for them.

How Do You Activate Forgiveness?

First you have to understand why. Why did they break your heart? Why did they leave you? Why did they cause the divorce? Just for a moment, put aside your judgment, and suspend any thoughts of blame. Cut through all the clutter and just look for the answer to why. The answer may not be rational. It may not be logical. It probably won't make sense. That's okay. You're just looking for the answer to, "Why?"

Is it because they weren't satisfied with you? Is it because you didn't make enough money? Or you weren't funny enough? Remember, the answer to why they left probably doesn't make sense, and you just want to get to the answer. Most people don't make decisions based on logic. They make decisions based on emotion.

Here's an example. My wife left because she wasn't happy – period. It has nothing to do with logic. From my perspective, she should have been happy. It had nothing to do with reason. Now, all these years later, she's still not happy. She's just not happy with someone else. You see, it really was something in her.

Years ago, I knew a dentist who was married to a woman named Michelle and they had two kids. They decided to build their dream house. By the time the house was complete, his wife was sleeping with the builder and she divorced the dentist.

The dentist told me he knew why his wife left. She was bored in their relationship and she was more attracted to the more macho builder.

On the other hand, I recently became re-acquainted with a woman who went to high school with my brother. She was married to a very macho ironworker. She had an affair with an accountant and divorced her husband, the ironworker.

So really, why did these two women leave their husbands? On a superficial level, you could say that they're opposites. One woman left a dentist for a more manly man and the other woman left a manly man for one with more money. But Michelle married the dentist, so there was obviously something about him that worked for her at some point in her life, and the second woman chose to marry the ironworker, so there was obviously something about him that worked for her.

As an outsider observing the situation, it's easy to see how the dentist in the first situation and the ironworker in the second situation were both devastated and felt betrayed. But can you also begin to see that it's not any flaw of the dentist or the ironworker that caused the divorce?

For the sake of simplicity, you could say the dentist's wife wanted a more macho man and the iron-worker's wife wanted a less macho man. The point is, each of those women knew the man they were marrying, but over time they became bored or disenchanted or unhappy and they decided they needed more of something or they needed something different.

Both the dentist and the ironworker were good men. Neither of their wives sought out marriage counseling, tried to fix the marriage or, for that matter, really ever told their husbands there was a problem. Instead, they pretended to be good wives while going behind their husband's back.

As I said, both men were devastated initially. But both of them came to realize that it wasn't them; it was their wife who wanted something more. They both came to realize that no matter how much money they had or how manly they were, it would never have been enough. In fact, they both came to realize that no matter who their wife married, it would not have worked out because in each case their wives focused on what they perceived they were missing or what they didn't have.

As an outsider it would be easy to tell the dentist, "It's not you; it's her." So for each of these guys, they figured out why she did it. The answer was simple. She felt like she was missing out on something and she believed she found it with the other man. She had to be with that other man.

Marriage is probably the most important relationship of your life. You swear an oath in front of all of your loved ones that you will commit your life to this person. Without being emotional, I think almost everyone would agree that you should go to great lengths to save your marriage, to solve the problems. Yet, some people abandon that commitment casually and betray the one person to whom they have sworn to be a life-long partner. By definition, anyone who would betray his or her lifetime partner is someone that a healthy person would not want to be in relationship with.

Whether the women in these examples were flawed or selfish, there are a lot of people who are just simply incapable of long-term loving, giving relationships. Whether you call them selfish, self-centered, or dysfunctional, they had a reason for leaving the relationship. It might not have been logical or fair, but they truly felt they had to do it. The more irrational the reason, the better you are without them.

Consciously Activate Faith

There's another part to this forgiveness thing that makes it even stronger. It's faith. Developing faith that things really do work out is absolutely necessary. You may not be able to see how it's going to work out from where you're standing right now, but that doesn't mean that it won't work out. There really is a bigger picture that we don't see. And the funny thing is, the more you develop faith, the more you will see things working out for you and your family. The more you stop trying to control everything in your life, the more you will find that your life makes sense and the more you will see the pattern.

I'm going to tell you a story about how a tragedy turned into something terrific – and every word of it is true.

There was a pretty young Italian girl engaged to be married. She and the groom made a handsome couple. Both families were looking forward to the marriage, and you can imagine how excited the young couple was.

Think of the thoughts that go through a young bride's mind a week before her wedding – the excitement, the hopes, the dreams. Can you imagine how that young woman felt when her groom-to-be was killed in a motorbike accident five days before the wedding?

That's a tragedy that most of us will never experience. I can't imagine there was any way to console her. Had I been there, I wouldn't have even tried to tell her that someday, something good could come from this. And yet, as Paul Harvey would say, "Let me tell you the rest of the story."

The best man, and best friend of the groom, was on an ocean liner coming from America back to Italy when the groom was killed. He didn't know the groom had died until he landed in Italy. He had never met the bride until this tragedy.

Over time the best man and the bride became friends, fell in love, and got married. (You saw that coming.)

I never knew the young bride, I only knew her as Nona, because that young bride was my great-grandmother. I only knew her as a little Italian lady who spoke broken English, pinched my cheeks until they hurt, and was always laughing and happy. And yes, the best man was my great-grandfather. They had six children and many grandchildren and great-grandchildren.

If she had married the original groom, I wouldn't be here. Neither would my mom, my aunt, my cousins, my children, and my grandchildren. Things have a way of working out.

How to Exercise Forgiveness

It's essential that you forgive your ex-spouse. Why? Because as long as you hold the grudge, it holds you back. When you hold a grudge against someone, when you refuse to forgive him or her, you have this invisible connection with him or her. It continues to give them power over you.

I'll give you a real-life example. Years ago, a woman I know followed her husband from New York to Arizona for his job. A couple years after they were out in Arizona, he started having an affair with a woman he'd met. My friend, of course, was the last to know.

Her husband would literally take this other woman on long holidays and charge it to the family credit card. Of course, he lied about it; he told his wife it was company business. The neighbors knew he was with someone else because he would send his wife home with their three small children to New York, and while they were in New York, he and the girlfriend were playing house at their home. Sound familiar? It happens all the time, but that doesn't make it right.

After their divorce, my friend had to leave her home in Phoenix, a place she had come to love, and move back to Buffalo, where she had never dreamed she would return. She began to raise her children by herself.

As you can imagine, this was quite a different life than she envisioned when she got married. Her ex-husband ended up getting married to the other woman and having children with her.

For a few years, his first wife couldn't forgive him. That's understandable. But look at it from the outside. He married the other woman, had two more kids and kept going to work everyday. She, on the other hand, had been a good wife and a great mom and what does she get in return for it? Betrayal. Humiliation. Being cheated on and lied to. She got to trade in her nice new house in Phoenix, Arizona for a small house she shared with her single cousin in Buffalo.

Unjust? You bet. Unfair? You better believe it.

For a short time she held a grudge. She was angry. Perfectly understandable. But what did it accomplish? Did it stop him from marrying again or having more children? No. Did it stop him from having a career? No. Unfair as it might seem, it stopped her. It stopped her from being fully present with her children. It stopped her from having a relationship with a good man.

Become Objective

And then one day she forgave him. Which does not mean in any way, shape, or form that she agrees with what he did or that she approves of it or condones it. It does not mean that what he did had any honor to it. Just the contrary. He had no honor, he had no integrity, and she knows that. They're not friends, and she doesn't care to be in his life. They live separate lives now. That's what divorce means: You each go your separate way.

She came to realize that the lack of honor and the lack of integrity was his problem, not hers. She came to realize that there really is karma or whatever you want to call it. She realized, truly, that what goes around comes around. She came to realize that it wasn't her place to punish him, even if she could, and of course she couldn't.

She came to realize that he had actually done her a favor because she was much, much better off without a man like that in her life. She came to realize that she had married a man who was basically selfish and self-centered and that in some weird way, she had known that even before she married him. But she married him anyway. She came to realize he was no happier with his second wife than he had been with her.

She came to realize that even though his second marriage lasted longer than the marriage with her, he was still searching for that something that was missing. He was still not satisfied.

Her kids would come home after a brief visit with their dad and talk about how Dad and their step mom were always bickering at each other. And while he would never admit that to her (because again, we're always concerned with looking good and not looking bad), she knew the kids were telling the truth.

She knew from having been married to him that he did have those selfish qualities and he did easily become frustrated. She could tell from the brief comments that the same issues she had with him were just being played out again with a different woman.

Arizona Lessons

My friend's divorce happened ten years ago. Her three kids know their dad, though he lives out of state and they've always spent time with him during school vacations. Can you imagine how many times she could have tried to poison their minds against their father? But she didn't. She was honest with them, and I strongly advise you to be honest with your children.

Her kids know their father had an affair. They don't remember it; they were too young at the time. But when they were old enough to ask, she told them the truth. They know the things their dad did. No embellishments, no accusations, just simple statements of fact.

They know their dad is selfish. They've seen it firsthand. People like that rarely change. The flaws he had, he still has. They don't hate him for it, they're not upset about it; it's just how he is. But remember, there are consequences to every action. There are consequences to his actions.

As a result of the things he's done, his children aren't as close to him as to their mother. It's not because she poisoned their minds. It's because they see who he is, and, while they love him, they'll always have a much greater love and respect for their mom because she earned it by being a great parent.

Are My Feelings Subjective or Objective?

If your feelings about your ex are only focused on him or her, they are subjective and not doing you one bit of good. Whatever issues your spouse had with you weren't solved because he or she left you. They may put on a good face because they especially want to look good in front of you. But most likely, their problems haven't gone away. Regardless of whether they have or not, it's not up to you to correct them.

What a shame to spend the next five years holding a grudge against your ex-husband or ex-wife only to find out five years from now that they have been miserable after all. The real shame is if you spend the next five years being upset and hurt, you will have missed out on the joy that you could share with your children.

Whether you're with your children one day a month or every day, you have an opportunity to create joy with them, to make lasting memories, to help form happy and healthy human beings.

That is why you must forgive her (or him). Regardless of the circumstances, you have some responsibility, even if it's nothing more than admitting you made a bad choice because you chose to marry this man or woman, and no one held a gun to your head.

So how do you become objective? How do you shift your perspective?

Becoming objective begins with taking a giant step backward and looking at the bigger picture. The smaller your thinking, the more subjective it is. The bigger your thinking, the better off you'll be.

Here's what I mean. Stop thinking just about yourself. Instead, include as many people as possible, include as many possibilities as possible, and include a wider timeframe. It's okay to think about yourself, but consider the possibility that in the long run, over the years, you will actually be better off not married to this person. Considering your lifetime as a whole is a much bigger perspective than just how you feel right now. Consider the possibility that your children will be better off in the long run.

I personally know many young adults who will honestly tell you that they are glad their parents divorced when they were young (although they may not have felt that way at the time). In hindsight, they would not have wanted to grow up in a house with Dad (or Mom, depending on the circumstances).

A soldier in the heat of a major battle has no idea if the battle is being won or lost. He may think that what he personally is doing is hopeless or meaningless. But if he could be transported behind the lines with the generals, then perhaps the battles would make sense to him. It's the same in business and sports and life. The bigger your perspective, the more things make sense. And the more things make sense to you, the less you will resist.

I have the benefit of hindsight, but I saw early on that my children and I were better off on our own. Will the same be true for you in the long run? The hurt is temporary and usually turns into a blessing. Once you see that it's a blessing, you're becoming objective.

A very smart man (my dad) once told me that there are no guarantees in life, so just look for the opportunities. Look for the opportunities that come from your divorce. A better environment for your children? A more happy home life? A partner that treats you better? A relationship with someone that enriches your life?

Life is ironic. Those could be the very blessings that come to you because someone hurt you.

Do You Want to be Right or Happy?

In my law practice, I've handled many business divorces. I'm always amazed at how a client can tell me how their former business partner is the devil in person.

The first time I handled such a case, I was very young, and for six months I believed everything my client told me. Then it dawned on me that he had been in business with his partner for over ten years. It's not that I didn't believe him after that; it's just that I realized he wasn't taking any responsibility for the situation.

In my own marriage, I married someone who was fundamentally different from me. In short, she's a negative personality and I'm positive. We had different values. In fairness, we were only nineteen years old when we met, and most nineteen-year-olds aren't that wise. Many of my friends who knew us when we were in college, told me after our divorce that she changed on me.

I sort of bought that for a while. They were telling me the truth as they saw it, but then I realized she hadn't really changed. She had always been that way. I either didn't see it or didn't want to see it when we were young.

The important thing here is to understand that when you forgive someone, what he or she did to harm you may still be wrong, but you have freed yourself from him or her. They no longer have the power to ruin your day. They no longer have the power to deny you the enjoyment of your children's company.

Earlier in this chapter, we mentioned the fact that it's so difficult for many people to forgive, and sometimes far more difficult for those who have a very strong moral grounding. In my opinion, this comes from the fact that they are brought up to understand the difference between right and wrong and are taught to do the right thing. At least that's a good system to learn.

As children, we're often punished for doing the wrong thing. We then grow up and from our point of view we pretty much always do the right thing and want to see people punished when they do the wrong thing, just as we were punished for doing them.

There Are Always Consequences

Life goes along fairly smoothly when suddenly, someone does you one great big wrong. It doesn't seem like they're punished for it while you have to suffer from it. You've been betrayed not once but twice. Your partner for life has betrayed you and then you've been betrayed by the system that taught you that wrongdoing is immediately punished.

However, it's important to remember: There are always consequences to our actions. Whatever he or she did or didn't do, there will be consequences. You may not see those consequences for years. You may never see them. However, just because you didn't see them doesn't mean they didn't happen.

My friend's husband who abandoned her in Phoenix, is now stuck in an unhappy marriage working at a job he hates. My friend is now happily married to a man she loves, living in a million-dollar house. She knows real love and real intimacy. She didn't know what she was missing, and there was no way she was going to learn it unless she went through the divorce. She also has the satisfaction of having raised those three little children who are now happy and healthy adults.

The consequences won't always be that obvious. The point is, you don't know how things are going to turn out. It's all a process, and you're not in competition with anyone.

Just let go of your bad thoughts about him. Forgive. However, I don't think you have to forget. In fact, I think you should remember. It helps you to grow and learn and avoid making the same mistake again. Forgiveness is a gift you give yourself.

More Help

If you need more help with this, go to our website at www.WisdomForDivorcedParents.com. There's an excellent CD there you can order that will guide you through an exercise that will help you set yourself free.

As the Eagles said in their song, *The Heart of the Matter*, "I think it's about forgiveness, even if, you don't love me anymore."

Chapter 4 - Things to Consider

❖ Forgiveness is for you, stupid!

❖ Activate forgiveness by understanding why.

❖ Develop faith by thinking of situations that "worked out" (i.e., the long run).

❖ Do you want to be "right" or happy?

❖ Blaming accomplishes nothing positive.

GETTING OVER IT

Chapter 5

It's All About Your Kids, And Time Is Short

"Bear in mind that the wonderful things you learn in your schools are the work of many generations. All this is put in your hands as your inheritance in order that you may receive it, honor it, add to it, and one day faithfully hand it on to your children." ~ *Albert Einstein*

There really is nothing new under the sun. Everything in this book has been taught before. In fact, you already know the concepts we're talking about. The point of the book is to serve as a gentle reminder to you to focus on those concepts and give you concrete examples specifically regarding raising children after or during a divorce.

How old are your kids? How many years will it be until they're sixteen or seventeen years old? How fast did the last five years go by?

The next five years will go by even faster, and with each year, your influence over your kids becomes less. Once they're about seventeen years old, your job is done. They are who they are going to be. They'll be grown up.

Once they're sixteen or seventeen years old, the foundation has been laid. There will be minor corrections and little changes, and hopefully they'll still listen to your advice. But remember, you can't re-do the foundation.

Really stop and think about how important this time is. Because what you're doing now will affect the person that they are when they're 30, 40, even 60 or 70 years old.

There are a whole lot of people in this world trying to overcome the issues of their childhood and there are plenty of gurus and self-help books telling them to live in the present, to forgive their parents for what they did, and on and on. They can't go back and re-live the past. But your children can flourish in their lifetime because it hasn't happened yet. You can make decisions that will help them the rest of their lives.

I'm not talking about how to be the perfect parent. That's not realistic. You'll make mistakes. I made mistakes. Your kids will have to overcome obstacles just as mine did.

But if you really want to be the most effective parent you can be, if you really want to give your kids every chance at happiness, then you have to take action now.

You have to have a system. Since you've read the first four chapters of this book, you're well on your way.

Effective Parenting 101: Be Accountable

In our culture, there are tons of books that talk about the fact that you must be accountable to yourself, that you are responsible for your own life, that you can create the world you want. Everyone mouths those words, but how many people actually do it? How many people really live that way?

Here's a real life example. My ex-wife is highly intelligent; she was an honor student in college. There is no doubt she understands intellectually that she is responsible for her own actions. I believe that, intellectually, she knows that she can't control me or anyone else. And yet, the one thing that stands out in my mind, probably more than anything, is how time and time again she would do something wrong and her response would be, "I can't help it." She knew that what she was doing was wrong, but she wouldn't admit it, and she certainly wouldn't accept responsibility for it.

I'm sure you know someone just like that. So why does a man repeatedly tell himself that he's not going to fight with his ex-wife, but then he does it again? Why is it that intelligent people who know they shouldn't commit adultery, still do? Why do good parents argue with their spouse in front of their children, even when they know they shouldn't? Why do adults talk bad about their ex in front of their children? They know it's not good for the kids.

You know that arguing with your ex over money or time spent with the kids is going to create pain for you and your children, but you can't help yourself. You know that arguing with your ex over school schedules, or who is going to pay for the doctor bill isn't going to help your kids, but you have to do it; you have to make a point.

How do you get past that? How do you change it? Do you really want to spend the next ten years fighting?

More importantly, do you want to spend the next ten years as an effective parent? When your kids are grown, will you look back and honestly tell yourself, "I did a pretty good job." Or will you look back and just make excuses like, "I made mistakes, but I just couldn't help myself."

Decide right now if you're going to be an effective parent or not. There really are no excuses. Either you teach your children the lessons they need to learn or you don't.

The Magic Formula

We've talked about the problems. Now, what is the solution and how do we get there? Here's the magic formula, and yes, it will take practice and you'll have set backs. But if you stick with it, you'll get there.

Step One: Get a New Trigger

Here's an example: Your ex-husband is now bringing your children around his new girlfriend when they're with him. She's the same girl that he was sleeping with while you were married to him. On top of that, he's not paying as much child support as he should be paying. That information is in your head all the time. When he stops by to see the kids and he says something inoffensive like, "I'm taking them to the movies," you jump all over him and there's a big argument in front of the kids. The kids are understandably upset, you're upset, and he feels like a victim because he hasn't done anything wrong.

It's completely understandable that you're angry. You've been betrayed, violated, lied to, and cheated. Of course that's not what the conversation was about – it was just about the movies. He doesn't understand why you reacted that way and more importantly, the kids don't get it.

We've all been exposed to enough pop culture to know that it comes from unresolved issues. From a practical point of view, we all live in our own minds. We have these conversations that go on all the time. You've just gone through a divorce, or you're just going through one and most of those conversations involve how bad he is, or how rotten she is, or what a victim you are. It doesn't take much to trigger an outburst. Sometimes it's just the sight of him. To the extent you've actually done what we talked about in the earlier chapters (i.e., be with it, forgive him, forgive yourself), those triggers will be greatly diminished.

Let's work on this a little bit more. What do I mean when I say develop a new trigger? Before you have a confrontation, before you see him, before you talk to her on the phone, train yourself to think of the big picture. Take the long view. Ask yourself if this is really going to matter in ten years. Maybe you've heard statements like that before, but here's an exercise that will help you apply it to your situation, because it's really not about whether it will matter to you in ten years. It's about whether it will matter to your son or daughter in ten years. Think of your son when he's eighteen years old and he's going off to college, or he's going to get his first apartment or first job. Think of your daughter when she's 25 years old and she's married and she's coming to visit you with her husband and new baby.

The actual age or circumstance is really up to you. Come up with something that works for you, some milestone that you can easily hold in your mind. Because yes, your little eight-year-old will one day, very soon, be eighteen years old.

Once you get that picture in your head of that eighteen-year-old boy or that 25-year-old woman, spend some time and think of the person you want them to be. What are their hopes and dreams? How healthy is their outlook on life? Will your eighteen-year-old boy have issues of anger because his dad left and his mom was always angry? Or will he be a healthy young man with a positive outlook on life, who is ready to take on life's many challenges because mom was always there with him – mentally, physically, and emotionally.

Who will your 25-year-old daughter be? Will she be a young woman that you look at knowing her marriage doesn't stand much of a chance? What effects will that have on her children? Or, will you see a young woman who is emotionally stable, can choose a good man, and knows how to give and receive love?

You need to pick the time and the scenario that feels right to you and it may be more than one setting. It just has to be something that's real to you, because ultimately that's your goal – healthy and happy children. No one's life is perfect and certainly no person is perfect, but you want to give your children the tools so they can successfully navigate through life and deal with the challenges, because they, like you, like all of us, will have challenges.

Step Two: Visualize Your New Trigger

When you have that picture firmly in your mind, then you've developed your new trigger. Now, when your ex-wife tells you she needs more money, or when your ex-husband says he's going to take the kids with him and his new girlfriend to the amusement park, you may still feel a twinge of anger.

Before that anger explodes like a volcano, you immediately go to your new trigger. Picture the strong young man who is going off to college or the pretty young woman who is bringing the kids over to visit grandma or grandpa. Then you ask yourself if it really matters in the long run if they go to the park with dad and his new girlfriend? Is that going to promote or hinder the really important goal – the healthy young adult?

I'm not saying give in to everything they want. This is really all about perspective. Step out of the day-to-day issues. You may want to yell at your ex-husband because he has a new girlfriend and perhaps your typical response is, "I can't help it." You know you really can help it. Do what's best for the kids in the long term, not what makes you feel better in the short term. If you tell your kids that their dad is a jerk, is that going to help your little boy turn out to be the man you want? If you tell them Mom caused the divorce because she's a liar, is that going to help your little girl turn into the woman you want?

You're no longer connected to him or her, but you do both have the same goal. You want your children to be successful in life. So find that trigger; find that vision in your brain. Keep that goal in front of you; make it an obsession. There will be times when you trip and fall; don't give up, just get back on the path.

Ah, but you say, I am doing that, but he still yells at me or she still gets irrational. So now you have a clear choice. What's more important to you – your short-term interest or your children's long-term interest?

Step Three: No One Admits They're a Jerk

When I was married, my wife would yell at me if I walked across the carpet in the living room after she ran the sweeper in there. Really. She was mad because I messed up the lines. You know, those lines you get when you run a sweeper over carpeting? She wanted to keep them nice and straight without footprints. True story.

She would get mad about all kinds of things that just didn't seem important to me. I haven't been in her house for years, but I'm guessing there are still lines in those carpets. Over the last few years of our marriage, we had many disagreements. I define disagreements as her yelling at me and me not really understanding what the big deal was about. She had a quick temper and she was quick to yell, so we had a lot of disagreements. Were they disagreements or arguments? Does it really matter? Sometimes, I would calmly explain my position to her and other times I would lose my temper and I would yell right back at her.

Then I stopped arguing with her. I simply wouldn't argue. I didn't give in; I would just tell her, "I don't think that's right" and I'd walk away. I'd stay calm. I wasn't trying to make her mad; it wasn't a new tactic. I had just realized in all the arguments we had, no one ever won a single argument. No one ever changed the other person's mind or viewpoint. She never once said to me, "You're right Len, I'm an asshole. I'm wrong and you're right."

Have you ever seen two people get all riled up, yell at each other, and then one of them suddenly just stops and says, "Hey you're right. I'm really a big jerk," or words to that effect? I've never seen it. I've never seen it in my personal life. I've never seen it in my professional life. I'm an attorney and I've handled hundreds of lawsuits and not once have I ever seen one party to the lawsuit say, "You know, I was really unfair to him and this is all my fault." I've never seen politicians do it, and I'm pretty sure you've never seen anyone do it either.

That's because we all have our own point of view and we have a hard time seeing the other person's point of view. Maybe the other person really is wrong. Maybe your ex-wife really is selfish and self-centered. Maybe your ex-husband really doesn't care about anyone but himself. Whatever their personality traits, they're not going to change. You don't have any control over them. You didn't have any control over them when you were married, and now you have even less control.

Step Four: Don't Fight

So what's the answer? Don't fight. You've already got a really good reason for not wasting your time with pointless arguments about what's in your children's best interest, but now you've got another good reason. It's ineffective. It doesn't work. I am not saying give in. I am not saying just roll over and be a wimp. What I am saying is do what's best for your children and for you. Live your life the way you want to based on your values and your principles and forget the rest. Because, in reality that's all you can do.

In the first chapter, we talked about being with it. We talked about accepting the bad things that had happened to you so you could release them. In a way, this is a mini version of the same thing. It still comes down to acceptance. There's an old saying that says it all. In fact, it's a refrigerator magnet I gave to my kids. "God, grant me the strength to change the things I can change, serenity to accept the things I cannot change, and the wisdom to know the difference."

Your ex-husband is not the devil. Your ex-wife is not a whore. If they were, you wouldn't have married them. They're just people who have a lot of insecurities and fears and are trying to figure out how to get through life.

I'm not making excuses for them. Chances are they really are wrong. But what's more important to you, being right or getting it right? Because getting it right means being an effective parent and raising children who have a shot at successful lives.

For some reason, we humans just like to be right. We want to feel vindicated. Life's ironic because we spend a lot of time wanting to be right and trying to prove that we're right and it doesn't matter to anyone but us.

I've heard many divorced people say to me, "Yeah, but my situation is different." These principles apply to everyone. What will give your life more meaning? Being right? Or raising healthy children?

Step Five: Take the Long View

Let me give you another example based on someone I know. A friend of mine is raising her two girls by herself. She's a single parent, because her ex-husband left her years ago for another woman when both of the girls were just babies.

He lives out of state and he's now on his fourth wife. He lives in a bigger, more expensive house than she does, drives nicer cars, and takes more vacations. He also pays only about half the child support that he should pay.

Realistically, she is the only parent because she handles the day-to-day responsibilities such as homework, and teaching them respect and responsibilities. Dad is just a fun guy they visit a couple of weeks every summer.

From an adult's perspective, this guy is a schmuck. From the perspective of those two young girls, most of their lives they have adored their dad simply because he's their dad and simply because he's never been there day-to-day to discipline them and do all the routine parenting chores. Those two young girls have often viewed him with admiration that an outsider would say he certainly doesn't deserve.

Their mom had the perfect opportunity to demean him. After all, she's with the girls everyday and Dad lives out of state. And don't forget, Dad is on his fourth wife and doesn't pay nearly the child support he's supposed to. But she didn't talk about him in derogatory terms. What good would come from telling those two girls that their dad was selfish and unable to sustain relationships?

On the other hand, she's been honest with them. They know Dad doesn't pay the support he should pay and they know he's on his fourth wife. Those are just facts. Don't make the mistake of lying to your children or hiding the truth from them. Some people think that they are protecting their children by making their ex seem to be a better person than they really are. If your husband left because he had an affair, the kids need to know that. They will find out one day, and they will resent you for having lied to them.

Now those two little girls are in their early teens and they see that Dad is ready to skip out on wife number four. Now they're starting to see their dad for who he really is. It's painful for them to realize that their dad is not that great man they thought he was. But he's not a great man, and there is no way he ever will be. It's important that they see him for who he really is. They will get past the hurt and they will still love him.

Step Six: Be Honest & Factual Without Blame

To deceive your children will only cause them pain and stunt their growth. If their mom had spent years berating their father, their natural inclination would have been to defend him. Ultimately, they would still come to the same conclusion; it just would have taken longer and caused more pain. On the other hand, if she had tried to cover up his faults and pretend he was some noble man, that also would have deceived the children and inhibited their growth.

All children, whether coming through a divorce or not, ultimately come to realize that their parents are just human beings. Sometimes parents, whether in a divorce situation or not, are a good role model for children on how not to live their lives.

As those two girls grow older, they will see more and more how their father lives his life and their mother lives her life, and they will naturally gravitate more and more toward her style of living. The Reverend Martin Luther King had it right: "The truth will set you free."

Stop and think about this example. My friend raising those two children could have done a lot of things. She could be upset with her ex; she could call him on the phone and yell at him; and she could talk badly about him in front of the children. Would it change him? We all know it wouldn't change him one bit.

Fortunately for her, she understands that, so she doesn't waste her energy trying to change what she cannot change. She's not a martyr about it and she's not looking for credit. She just simply keeps marching, one step at a time, toward her goal – raising healthy young children.

As I mentioned earlier, I have a good relationship with my daughters, but I have also encouraged them to have a good relationship with their mom. I don't candy coat it. I don't cover up her issues. We talk openly and honestly about things. I simply didn't want my children to grow up to be selfish or self-centered.

Once again, take the long view. This is really important. It's not a competition. Children will not win if Mom and Dad are competing for them.

Spirituality: Following Your Inner Voice

All of us have two competing voices in our head pulling us in opposite directions. What we call the ego is that part of our mind that is all about looking out for Number One. It's that part of us that's always concerned with protecting ourselves or getting our fair share. When the ego is out of control, that's when we are selfish or self-centered because we feel that we're alone and we have to protect ourselves. That's when we start to rationalize.

Fortunately, there's another part of our minds. That's the part that knows there is something greater than each and every one of us. Whether you call that something God, or the creative force, or love, on some level we all know we are all connected. We all have an inner voice that tells us the right thing to do. Follow that inner voice; stay connected to it. That's where your answers lie.

That's why when someone does something selfish they say, "I had to do it." Even the most selfish person recognizes there is a better way to do it and that there's a right way and by saying, "I had to do it," they're acknowledging they didn't take the right path.

Some people refer to it as karma. Some just talk about how what goes around comes around. I simply think of it as being connected to Spirit. Do the right thing by your kids and it will pay off for you, for them, and for generations to come.

Children Gravitate to the Healthy Parent

A friend of mine is a psychologist who once told me when my children were young that children will naturally gravitate to the healthy parent. Here's a real world example: I've been divorced many years. Over the years, my former spouse has told my children that, "Your dad is not really the good guy he makes himself out to be."

She doesn't always attack me, but every so often she'll say things to them to try to harm my relationship with them or their relationship with the woman I now love.

So, should I wring her neck? Should I attack her? There were certainly times when I wanted to. Would it be effective to go yell at her? Would it promote my ultimate goal of raising two fine, young, healthy women who are emotionally stable and know the difference between right and wrong?

So what happened? Well, those little girls who were six and eight when we split up, are now 22 and 24. Being the proud dad I am, I could rave about how wonderful they are – and they really are. They're everything that I had hoped for. They love their mom. I want them to love their mom, and I've always encouraged that. It's healthier for them. They see her on a regular basis. They're also clear about who she is. They know she loves them, but they also know she's difficult and selfish. When mom gets upset, they don't get caught up in her drama, because they see who she is.

My daughters are closer to me than they are to their mom. You might read that last sentence and think I'm proclaiming some kind of victory over my ex-wife. I am not. I have never felt that I'm competing with my ex-wife for the affections of our children. I have never felt that I'm competing with my ex-wife for anything. We both have the same goal: raising healthy young adults.

When I say my children are close to me, I'm not bragging. It's an important point. That situation came about, not because of lying or manipulating or forcing. In fact, all of those things will bring the opposite result. The reason my children are closer to me is because I was honest, loving, and refused to diminish my ex to them. Children are smart. They figure it out. You can't fool them in the long run, even if they believe you for a while.

More Help

Two final thoughts. If you want more help on this, I would strongly recommend you look into taking a class called *The Landmark Forum*. Their website is www.LandmarkEducation.com. This class is intense and takes an entire weekend. It's also not cheap, but it's well worth it.

I would also strongly recommend that you meditate. It's a very simple practice that can be as brief as ten minutes a day, and I guarantee it will change your life when you get into the habit of meditation. That's the only way you'll do it. You have to make it a habit. I would suggest meditating every morning when you first wake up or every night before you go to bed.

Chapter 5 - Things to Consider

❖ Visualize the future you want for you and your children.

❖ What can you do today to move toward that goal (think only about today).

❖ When is the last time you heard someone in an argument admit they were wrong?

❖ Be honest with your children without "blaming".

❖ Listen to the answers inside you.

GETTING OVER IT

Chapter 6

Say What You Mean And Mean What You Say

"When I do something in my family because I really enjoy it, then my duty has become my pleasure. And it is a pleasure for all the people around me."
~ Dr. Jess Lair

Stop right there. Don't gloss over this. Everyone assumes they can communicate. Before you skip over this chapter, ask yourself when was the last time the little voice in your head was talking to you and you were supposedly listening to someone else? When was the last time you were discussing something with someone else – a child, co-worker or ex-spouse – and while they're talking a little voice in your head is putting together the arguments for your position?

What we discuss in this chapter will be specifically directed to communication with your children, but in reality applies to all the relationships in your life. And since your children are the most important relationship in your life, start with them.

Here are some simple rules.

Establish Trust: Be Your Word

Everything you say to your children is a promise or an agreement. Do what you say you're going to do and you build trust. Trust is what carries you through when they're sixteen years old and driving around with their friends and you don't know what they're doing.

I'm a sports fan, and there was a recent article about the Florida football team, which was about to go into the National Championship game against the Ohio State Buckeyes. Florida had a new coach named Urban Meyer. Everyone agreed he had turned the program around. All the players interviewed agreed the previous coach was a good coach. In other words, he knew how to call the plays, he knew what formation players should be in at what time, etc. But they were all really excited about this new guy and, in fact, with this new coach, their season had dramatically improved, even though they essentially had the same talent and a similar schedule. So what was the difference?

To a man, they all emphasized that the new coach had built a greater sense of trust among the players and coaches by using trust-building techniques. There were things like practices at midnight and certain competitions he had dreamed up. But the important point was that he had created a high level of trust.

As I've said before, we are repeatedly going to emphasize thinking in the long term.

Your children will be tempted and you won't be there looking over their shoulder so you have to instill character in them. And the first step in instilling character in your children is that they see character in you. It's simple. You are their role model. Whether you want to be or not, you are their first role model and probably their most important one.

Your kids don't need you to be the most fun parent on the block. What they need is a parent that can guide them, teach them and lead them. They need a parent who can show them how to live; they need a parent they can trust. You have to have character. The first step in having character is having integrity. Be your word.

Whenever you take an action that affects them or that they observe or are aware of, you are essentially telling them that it's okay to be that kind of a person. If you make excuses for failing to do something, you're telling them its okay for them to make excuses.

Like everything else about parenting, it's long term. It's decision after decision, moment to moment, day after day.

I find the easiest way to keep my focus is to ask myself, "What kind of adult do I want them to be?" Then, act on that.

Make Rules, then Enforce Them

One quick way to establish trust is to establish rules. Do this with the input of your children. It depends on their age, but sit down with them and let them know there are rules in your house, rules in their relationships. With their input, establish those rules. Make sure the rules are clear and that everyone agrees to them. This is important: Let them know the rules are not a burden. Teach them that the rules are a bonus, a benefit. Let them know that rules are a good thing because that way we each know what is expected of us and what we expect of others. Let them know that rules will help them achieve what they want. You have to adjust it to their age, but you get the idea. This also helps establish responsibility, as we'll discuss more in the next chapter.

Your kids don't need you to be the most fun parent or more fun than Mom. They need a parent who can guide them, a parent they can trust. Be careful what you say and how you live.

No Excuses: Be 100% Responsible

Having integrity means being 100% responsible for everything in your life. It means giving up your reasons and your excuses.

Every truly successful person I know lives their life as though they are 100% responsible for everything in their life. At first blush, many people think this is ridiculous or unrealistic. Other people kind of get the concept but they don't really live it.

Like other concepts in this book, while it may at first sound like a burden, in reality it's freedom.

When you really get that you are 100% responsible for everything in your life, it's a tremendously freeing experience because it allows you to create your life.

Think about it. If you're not responsible, if you don't have control over your own life, then you're just a victim, and whatever makes you unhappy will always make you unhappy because you can't change it, or get rid of it. I know you can see this truth.

This isn't about fairness or justice. It's about the law of cause and effect. Here's an example: A friend of mine said to me, "I don't buy that bit about you're 100% responsible for your life and you can create your own life. I've got a job and a boss I don't like, but I can't quit because I need the money."

What he doesn't understand is that he chose that job. His reply, of course would probably be, "Well, I needed the money." But the reality is he needs the money because of the choices he made. This particular individual doesn't live an excessive lifestyle. He simply needs the money because he chose to get married, he chose to have children, and he has responsibilities. He would reply, "Well I got married when I was too young and too dumb to know any better."

Get the point? He still caused all of this to happen. He made the choices. As I said, it's not about fairness or justice; it's about cause and effect. And I will be the first one to tell you that many of the most important decisions we make in life, we make without really having all the facts in front of us. Nonetheless, he brought the situation about, and, more importantly, he can change it. I'm not saying we can all be Bill Gates, but my friend has skills and talent and he could get a different job, one that he likes better. It might require him to accept less money, but he could cut back in certain areas of his life.

My friend hates his job but he could get a different job. A new job might mean he would have to move. It might mean less pay. Less pay means he would have to give up his boat, maybe even his golf league. Essentially, he's working at a miserable job so he can continue to go boating and golfing. That's what I mean about creating your own life. He is in reality choosing a miserable job.

He's not really being responsible for himself and his own life. It doesn't even sound like he's making excuses; he just appears to be stuck in a rotten job because he has a family to support. As long as that family's basic needs are met, I would suggest to you that his family would be happier if he were happier, even if he had to take a pay cut.

We all can get very creative in covering up our excuses. The corollary to this is that you do have complete control over how you react to any situation or any person.

Remember, you are the role model, so what do you want your children to see? What do you want them to model? What do you want them to be? Do you want them go through life making excuses? Great explanations for why they failed? Or do you want them to grab life with their hands and say, "I can do whatever I want to do. I am the master of my own destiny."

Sometimes people wimp out on this one because they argue, "If that were true, if I could do anything I wanted, then I would wake up tomorrow and I'd start a new job making a million dollars a year." That's not what we're talking about. What we are talking about is that if you have financial problems, you have the ability to make more money than you make now – probably a lot more. But you would have to make changes and you would have to do it in increments.

You might have to find a new job or get further education. You might have to seek out a mentor. You might have to learn a skill you don't already have. But they take effort and focus, and for a lot of people it's just easier to sit on their butt, watch TV, and whine. It doesn't make you a bad person; it's just a choice.

What kind of person do you want to be? And what kind of person do you want your children to be?

One more thought: I have a friend who grew up very poor in an abusive home environment. By the age of 40, he was a multimillionaire. He started out with no money, no connections. He never did get much of an education. To my knowledge, he's never cheated any one. He treats everyone with respect. He's bright, but I know many people who are smarter than him. He never won anything; he never had anything handed to him. He started with nothing and now he has everything - a wife and children, millions of dollars. He travels to beautiful places, he has interesting friendships, and he has a lot of fun.

I have another friend who also grew up very poor. Also had no connections, also never even knew his real dad, also never won anything or had anything handed to him. This guy is also worth millions. He has his own successful business. He never married and has no children (his choice). He also has no special talents nor is he especially brilliant. In fact, although he did graduate from college, I know college was difficult for him.

In many ways, these two men have nothing in common with each other. While they're both friends of mine, they have never met each other and I don't think they even know the other exists.

But there are two qualities they each possess and it's the same two qualities in each of them, and these two qualities are really obvious about them.

Never Make Excuses

The number one quality they each possess is that they never, ever make excuses. They have each had many failures. The same thing is true for each of them; they always come back believing that they can create their own success.

Imagine that. Do you know anyone like that? No matter what happens, not if it's a personal bankruptcy or losing a business, not if it's a project that failed — I've never heard them make an excuse. I've never heard them whine or feel sorry for themselves. Just something to think about.

Be Genuine

The second quality each of these men possesses is that they are genuine. Being genuine means being straightforward in your communications and take what you get. This means don't use force or manipulation as a way of trying to get what you want.

In earlier chapters, we talked about the fact we can't control other people. When you really understand that and accept it, you'll stop trying to manipulate or force others into achieving the results that you want, which, at best, will only get you a temporary result. Human beings always resist force and manipulation. Force and manipulation are really a product of fear.

When my children were young and they told their mom they wanted to live with Dad all the time, her response was to tell them that if they did that, she would disown them. Obviously, I knew she wouldn't disown them and I told them that. But she got what she wanted temporarily. They went back to live with her for a month. But, they realized Mom wasn't really going to leave them and then they moved into my house permanently.

What did she accomplish? More importantly, what did the kids learn? They learned that Mom doesn't really mean what she says. They learned she tried to manipulate through intimidation. Even small children know to resist force and manipulation. It's in our DNA.

Remember that you're the role model. We all know people who are manipulative and mean-spirited. I don't know anyone like that who is happy or content. Be what you want your children to be.

Be Free: Learn to Give Up Being Right

When I say give up being right, I'm not saying forget about the concept of right and wrong. It's incredibly important to teach your children the difference between right and wrong.

Giving up being right really relates to the whole idea of control. More specifically, it deals with the fact that you don't control anyone else. If you're having an argument with your ex or you're mad at them because you're right and they're wrong, this has nothing to do with making them right and you wrong. It has nothing to do with forgetting about right and wrong. It doesn't mean that you have to give in to them. It just means you aren't going to convince them that you're right. It just means, let it go. Again, think long term. Think what will be effective and what your kids are seeing as you interface with your ex.

They're wrong, you're right. Okay. So what does it matter?

They're not going to change. You've had a calm, logical discussion with them, maybe even one not so calm. The bottom line is they don't see it your way and they're not going to change. You're choice is simple and you only have two options: Be upset about it or let it go. If it's something that's so wrong it endangers the health of your children, then there are legal remedies you can pursue.

So really the question boils down to, "Do you have a remedy? Is there something you can pursue?" If the answer is yes, then the next question is: "Are you willing to pursue that remedy?" If the answer is still yes, then do that. As an example, your ex-husband may not be paying enough child support. There are legal remedies for that. If you want to pursue those legal remedies, you can.

On the other hand, if this is something over which you have no control, you simply cannot change it – or even if you can, you're not willing to commit to the change, then you still have two choices: Be upset about it because you're right, or, let it go. And that's where most issues lie.

Giving up being right really comes down to the fact that you learn to accept that other people don't do things the way you would do them, don't see things the way you see them.

Here's an example from my own family that has nothing to do with divorce but makes the point. Let's call my cousin Jerry. Jerry is a great guy to go out and have a beer with. He's fun loving, he laughs a lot. I've never heard him say anything bad about anyone. But Jerry drives his parents crazy because he is Lazy with a capital L. He has absolutely no ambition. He has above-average intelligence and he could have done something with his life. Jerry is in his 40's and he hasn't had a steady job in fifteen years. He's married to a woman who is just like him. Neither of them has had a real job for as long as anyone can remember. They get disability payments, welfare payments, food stamps. We don't even know what all they get. We don't know how they survive. Yet they seem to live fairly comfortably. Their house is a pigsty. They generally sit around all day eating and watching daytime TV.

Jerry's parents are the complete opposite – hardworking, never miss a day's work, rock-solid, salt of the earth. Their house is clean; they're unselfish. They have all those good qualities we all admire. Not only that, but Jerry has two brothers and a sister, also like the parents. So his entire family is clean cut, hardworking, all American, and Jerry is the exact opposite. Same family raised in the same environment, so how did Jerry turn out so bad? Who knows?

For years, my aunt and uncle would repeatedly get upset. Jerry was the black sheep of the family on so many levels. He did so many things that were wrong.

Finally, Mike, one of Jerry's brothers, gave up being right. He just let it go. He realized that on one hand, yeah, Jerry is wrong; he's just wasting his life. But, on the other hand, it's his life to waste. He's still lazy, he still lives in a pigsty, and still doesn't have a job. He'll probably always be that way, but there's no longer any animosity between him and his brother. Mike just accepts that's how Jerry is.

I don't think Mike ever visits Jerry at his house because he doesn't like that environment, and he probably doesn't do as many things with Jerry as he does with his other brother. But they do occasionally get together for a beer and when they do they enjoy each other's company.

At some level, Mike would like Jerry to change and be normal, but hc has acccpted the fact that is never going to happen. So instead of being upset with him and not having a relationship with Jerry, he has accepted what Jerry has crafted as his norm. He's accepted what is, so now he has a relationship with his brother that, in its own way, is normal and healthy.

Again, this concept applies to all the relationships in your life. Think about whether there is a relationship in your life that you have limited because you're right and they're wrong.

Do you see how this also ties in to our earlier discussion about you being responsible for everything in your life? You have the power to heal relationships. My cousin Mike healed the relationship with Jerry by giving up being right, by just accepting Jerry as he is.

Almost every family has someone like Jerry and some families have more than one. They just can't figure out why they are the way they are. Here's the message: Stop trying. Jerry was never going to be able to fix himself or heal his relationships with the rest of his family for whatever reasons.

On almost every issue, he's wrong and they're right. But Mike was smart enough or enlightened enough to realize that he could create a good relationship with his brother Jerry. Mike improved his own life, he eliminated some of the stress and some of the turmoil.

So whether it's your ex-spouse, your brother, your mother, or your boss, give up being right. You will see an instant improvement in that relationship. Once you do that, you'll actually get kind of excited about this new power that you found. You'll be able to use this new power to improve the conditions of your life.

Most importantly, it will have two positive effects on your children: (1) the more healthy relationships you show them, the better off they are and (2) one day you'll be able to pass that power on to them because you teach by doing.

Be a Courageous Communicator

Always deal with issues with your children head-on. My daughters told me throughout high school that their friends were always amazed at all the things they could talk to me about. They would say things like, "Mary can't believe I talked to you about that." Of course, I was forced into this because there was no mom around. The result is that my kids can talk to me about anything – sex, drugs, rock-n-roll. However, our goal here is to raise these children so they become productive and healthy young adults.

When my daughter was a freshman in high school she was the captain of the cheerleading squad. Very cool for a young girl. I mean let's face it, that's as good as it gets for a high school freshman girl. That's the path to popularity. Not only that, you're almost assured that you're going to be a cheerleader for the rest of your time in high school.

Well, the very next year when the cheerleading tryouts came around, I was very surprised when my daughter told me she was not going to be a cheerleader anymore. I was a little surprised because I thought she liked it, so of course we talked about it and she explained to me that she did like cheerleading. But, she didn't much care for a lot of the girls whom she figured would end up being on the squad.

Unfortunately, some of those girls were using drugs and doing things that you would definitely not want your young daughter doing. Suffice it to say, they set the stereotype of the really nasty cheerleader-type girls. These girls hadn't done anything mean to my daughter. Just the opposite, they were essentially inviting her into their club.

At a young age, she was able to resist some pretty powerful peer pressure. She made that decision on her own. It was a courageous decision. Lots of young people everyday make courageous decisions to reject peer pressure. But they need your parental help to do that; they need your strength and support. And they will know they have that strength and support; they will know they have that bedrock at home when they know that you trust them, when you listen to them, when you communicate with them.

When you communicate clearly and openly with your children and develop trust they will come to you with the important issues in their life. Be their guide. You are their anchor. You want them talking to you, not their friends.

Be Peaceful

This comes back to being accepting about what you're really trying to achieve. Don't take the easy way out. Develop an early warning system. What are the things in your relationship with your children that irritate, aggravate, or anger you? Think about what it is that really angers you.

Whatever you think it is, it really isn't that. Now you think I'm talking nonsense. Let me give you an example. When my daughters were in high school I used to get really aggravated when they would leave the bathroom a mess. Typically, they would spend hours in the bathroom, doing what girls do, so that they could leave and be beautiful and get to that party. They would make a half-hearted attempt to clean up the bathroom and boom, they were out the door. I'd go upstairs, take one look at the bathroom and become angry because the sink was a mess and the towels were just lying on the floor.

On its face, I was angry because they left the bathroom a mess. When I really analyzed it, I knew I was mad at myself because I was failing as a parent to modify their behavior. That's what I mean when I say, look at whatever it is that upsets you, and whatever you think it is, it's not really that.

It all ties together. Being peaceful also goes along with being 100% responsible for everything in my life. Being a parent is hard work and sometimes you get tired. I was just being too lazy to do what I knew needed to be done to change their behavior. So I counted to ten, went for a walk around the block and got peaceful. Once I put the responsibility on my shoulders, there wasn't anything to be mad about. There was no need to be upset.

Looking at things with a different perspective, the problem was simple. They're the children; I'm the parent. I had rules, one of which is to pick up the towels and clean the bathroom. They didn't follow the rules. Why should I get upset? What did getting upset accomplish? Did it change their behavior? If you have teenagers, you know that when you get upset they may avoid you, but they aren't really too concerned about you. What they are really concerned about is the consequences.

So the solution was simple. I called them on their cell phones. (I got them cell phones so I could reach them and they could report in to me.) I told them to come home and pick up the towels that were on the bathroom floor. They were mortified! They were half way across town in the middle of a party having fun. They couldn't believe my outrageous request. I remained completely calm and said with a smile in my voice, "Come on home. I'll see you soon. Goodbye." Now, I'm pretty sure as they were driving home from that party

I wouldn't want to hear what they were saying about me.

They came home, didn't say a thing, gave me dirty looks, went upstairs, cleaned the bathroom, and went back to the party. I just smiled. They always picked up the towels after that.

Be Inspiring

Don't be cynical; be inspiring. Act in a way that they are touched and that you make a difference in their lives. One final word on responsibility: Successful parents are responsible. Responsibility in this context is not a burden. It's not something you have to do, like pay the bills. It's not about fault or blame. It's not about guilt or shame. It's not about getting credit. It's not about judgment or what's right or wrong. It's not about what's good or bad.

Being responsible means being willing to deal with a situation in your life from the view that you are the creator of your life and of what you do. No one makes you responsible and you don't make anyone else responsible. It's a gift you give yourself.

Pass this lesson on to your children. Teach them to be responsible for themselves. Again, not a burden - acknowledge that they determine the consequences of their lives.

Here's an example of what happened in our family. My youngest daughter was an A/B student through grade school and into the beginning of high school. She hit a point where she just wasn't that interested in school. She got to that phase where doing homework was a struggle, and we started to have a little bit of friction because I just couldn't seem to get her motivated. I got one of those interim reports that showed her grades were falling. Boy, was I upset. I was really going to lay into her. She could see the tension in me, and suddenly I could see the defenses go up in her before a word was even spoken.

Something made me stop. I went for a walk around the block. (When you have daughters, it's wise to do that.) I calmed down and I think God inspired me. As soon as I approached her, I saw her tense up and her defenses were right there, ready to go. She knew I was going to yell, but I surprised her. I took a different approach.

Again, I was very calm. I just told her how much I loved her and how much I wanted to see her get the things she wanted in life. I told her in a couple of years she would want to go off to college and that right now her grades were good enough to go to probably most of the colleges that she would want to go to. In fact, if she wanted to go to the college where her sister was headed, she could probably get into that college, too.

On the other hand, if her grades started to slip, well, then she probably wouldn't be able to get into the college she wanted to and if that happened she'd probably come to me with tears in her eyes and ask me if I could help and unfortunately, I would have to tell her I wouldn't be able to help. Not that I didn't want to, I just didn't have the power to open those doors.

I reminded her that we had a pretty nice house and a pretty nice life. We took a vacation to the beach every year that they loved. They liked the house and the neighborhood. But I reminded her that it was my house. It didn't necessarily mean that one day she would have a house like that, and I reminded her that I was paying for the vacations and that didn't mean she would necessarily be able to afford vacations like that. I told her that my life was already established and I didn't want her to be confused, that she had yet to establish hers and that she could create the kind of life she wanted, but it was up to her.

I didn't say any of this with sarcasm or an attitude. I didn't say it to manipulate her. I didn't say it to get what I wanted. I said it with honesty and sincerity. She knew I was saying it to her because I loved her and I cared about her and I wanted what was best for her. But no matter what I wanted for her, it was up to her to choose how she would live her life. And a remarkable thing happened. All the tension in her just disappeared and I could see the defenses and the arguments and the justifications for why she had gotten bad grades just fly right out of her. Instead, she admitted she hadn't been trying.

The funny thing is, years later I mentioned that discussion to her and she doesn't even remember it. After that discussion, she accepted responsibility for all of her school work through high school and on through college. Now she did not become a 4.0 student. That's not her style. But she wanted to be a teacher and she wanted to get into a particular college that had a very highly respected teaching program. That college had certain requirements in order to be admitted. She learned what those requirements were and she met them. Next summer, she'll graduate from that college as a full-fledged teacher. This is the only career she ever wanted. By being responsible, she created that career for herself.

Take Nothing Personally

In all of your relationships, in all of your communications, take nothing personally.

Observe the world around you. Notice how often people get offended. Look for it. As an experiment, see how many times you can notice someone being offended in a single day. The more you observe it as an outsider, the more comical it becomes. People act like little kids.

Don't be like everyone else. Step back and be an observer. Watch how people interact with each other. You'll find it humorous. Think about all the times you've seen people in cars honk at someone else because they're upset or offended. People honk because someone pulls out in front of them and they honk because the other driver is going too fast or too slow. They really take it personally, as if the other guy is out to get them. Their rational mind knows that this stranger in the blue car really isn't out to get them, but we almost all act based on our emotions. People are offended because they think they're being attacked in some form. And once you feel you're being attacked, you're now justified to attack right back.

To a large extent, being offended arises out of faulty assumptions. People assume their ex is out to hurt them.

People assume that the cop who is giving them a ticket is just too full of himself. People assume that their co-workers are rude when there aren't enough chairs at the lunch table. It goes on and on and on.

You definitely should not assume anything when you're communicating with your children and you definitely should not be offended. There will be times when they do want to offend you. That's because they're trying to provoke or manipulate you. Don't play the game.

When you allow yourself to be offended, you also allow yourself to be manipulated.

I often deal in a world of lawyers. Talk about egos and people who are easily offended! I have to admit that on several occasions, I have used that against them in negotiations. I can't resist; it's just too easy to push their buttons. When you're easily offended, it's like wearing a big sign on your back that says, "I am insecure."

The easiest way out of this trap is to remind yourself to step out of the situation and be on the alert for other people becoming offended over silly little perceived slights.

In a sense, be a student of human psychology. Study other people. Just observe them – that's all that's required. As I said, you'll see it so often it will become humorous to you. The more you observe it in other people, the more humorous it is, the funnier it becomes, and the more quickly you'll realize when you're doing it, and you'll be able to stop.

Chapter 6 - Things to Consider

❖ Build trust with your children by always being honest.

❖ Most people think rules are inhibiting; in reality, they set you and your children free.

❖ The good news is, you're responsible for what happens in your life. The really good news is, that means you get to create your life.

❖ Be genuine.

❖ Be free by learning how to give up "being right".

❖ When you're angry with your kids – you're really angry about something else. Learn what that is.

❖ Learn how to take nothing personally.

Chapter 7

There Is No Tomorrow

*"You will either step forward into growth
or you will step back into safety."*
~ Abraham Maslow

There is no tomorrow. There is no yesterday. There is only today.

More specifically, there is only now. Think about it.

Nothing really happens tomorrow. You might think about something that's going to happen tomorrow but when it actually happens (whether it's how you expected or not), it's happening now.

This may be a silly example, but imagine you're in a spaceship a million miles from earth and you're observing our tiny, blue planet spinning.

Intellectually, you know people are getting up and going to work while others, on the other side of the planet, are going to bed. You understand they are experiencing a change of time. For you, there is no time. There is only now. That's why time travel is impossible. There really is no place to go to.

Small children instinctively understand this. For a small child, either Daddy is there or he's not. As we become grown-ups and become more sophisticated, we understand this idea of time.

So why am I talking about time travel in a book on parenting? What I really want to emphasize is that wherever you are with your children or whenever you are with your children, be totally with your children. Looking back on raising my children, one of the things I am the most proud of is that I was emotionally there for my children.

How about an example? I was recently divorced. I had to deal with the fact that my wife, the mother of my children, didn't want me anymore. At the same time, my career was taking off. My mind was filled with thoughts about the past and the future. My thoughts about the past focused primarily upon the fact that my marriage failed. This woman with whom I had children didn't want me anymore. It was a blow to my ego and my pride. It was painful. It caused me a great deal of fear, not for me, but for my children. What harm would come to them emotionally because they came from a broken home?

On top of all that, after years of hard work, my career was starting to take off. My business was growing. That would require effort and thought and nurturing to keep it going. As if that wasn't enough, I was now a single parent. So I had a lot of thoughts in my head about the past and I had lots of thoughts about the future. There were days when I was living in the past. There were other days when I was living in the future. But, as we discussed, there really is no past and there really is no future. Everything happens now.

If I'm living in the past dwelling on pain and failure, accusations and what ifs, I'm not really living my life. What's done is done. And if I'm worried about the future (how will my business turn out, will I meet the right woman, etc.) then I'm still not living my life. I'm not with my children. For that matter, I'm not with anyone. I'm just living in my mind.

So how do we live in the present?

The answer is simple. It usually is. Forgive, have faith, let go of the past. We already know these answers. It's the doing that's difficult.

I don't have a Ph.D. I'm not a child psychologist. I'm just someone who's already been where you're headed. Now let me tell you what worked for me.

Begin With The End In Mind

We discussed in a previous chapter that your primary goal as a parent is to give your children the tools that they can use to lead happy, healthy and successful lives. That's all that matters. That is your magnificent obsession. I'm not talking about doting on them or giving them everything they want. I'm talking about taking a long view of most of your decisions. I'm talking about recognizing the fact that what you are after is a great long-term outcome, but that it's built on a countless number of small steps.

Remember in the earlier chapter we talked about developing a new trigger, about seeing that little boy as an eighteen-year-old going out and getting an apartment, or seeing that little girl as a new mom? Whatever that vision is for you, keep that in your mind.

Move a Mountain One Stone at a Time

Every culture has sayings like that, because it's true. We live in a world where everyone wants instant gratification. Much about our culture is quick and instant.

We want it now. We are not taught patience.

As a parent, you must be patient and you must persevere. You don't need to think of this as a long battle that will wear you out. Instead, think of it as a privilege to raise children and the most important thing you will ever do with your life. You're not going to teach them all the things they need to know in one day, so settle in and enjoy the ride. Create a mindset that this is the one thing in your life that you're going to take your time on.

Remind yourself each day of the goal you're working toward and that it doesn't happen in a single day.

There will be days when you feel like you're off track and it's just not working. Don't give up. You don't know what the future holds. Keep the end in mind.

Your Influence Is Greatest Every Day

Teaching is what you do every time you interact with your children. And it always happens today. Whether you're helping with homework, going to watch a basketball game, or sitting down to have dinner, you are teaching them. It doesn't matter if you're having dinner in your kitchen or if you're a part-time parent who is having dinner at McDonald's. What matters is that you're really there. You are a guide and an anchor. Know that you are a teacher, that you are a role model. That's how you will have the greatest impact on your children. Parenting isn't about stirring speeches or big events. It's about the quiet times and the little things.

It's not uncommon in a divorce for one parent to be doing the real parenting – all the little stuff, day in and day out. Buying the groceries, helping with homework, monitoring their computer use, etc. And sometimes the other parent is mostly concerned with the big events. You know those events – being front-and-center for their birthday party, buying them jewelry from your latest trip, but never buying them tennis shoes.

If you're the Big Event Type, ask yourself if what you're doing is for you or for your kids? Are you doing the showy things to make yourself look good and ignoring what really matters? If you are, I've got a news flash for you – it doesn't make you look good. Your fifteen-year-old doesn't really need diamond earrings. It's not a competition. There's really only one question that matters. Are you contributing effectively to the upbringing of your children? If you really feel the need to do the showy things, go ahead, but make sure you also contribute in little ways. The stuff that really matters to your children are the things that no one sees.

On the other hand, if you're a parent who is really conscious about parenting, good for you, keep it up. Don't feel sorry for yourself. Being a good parent is truly its own reward. You are doing important work. It's the most important job you will ever have. I have clients that have tens of millions of dollars, but they cannot buy what you have.

So remember, you influence your children every day. Make it a point to teach them something positive each day.

Listen To Them; You'll Be Amazed

This is the essence of being with them. When that little voice in your head is rattling on incessantly about the past or the future, or coming up with an answer to what you think they're saying, you're not really hearing what they say. Experts tell us that 90% of communication is non-verbal. I'm sure that 90% number is an educated guess. But you and I both know most communication is non-verbal, and if you're not present with your children, they know it. What is the message you're telling them if you're not present? They're not worthy? They're not important? They're not valuable?

If you're in the bleachers at a peewee football game or a swimming meet, it's okay for your mind to wander. But when you're with your kids, you need to really listen to them. Everyone knows this, but it's sometimes hard to do and, of course, we're not always going to get it right.

Stop. Look. Listen.

I have a simple rule – Stop. Look. Listen. That means stop what you're doing, stop watching the TV, stop reading the paper, stop thinking about other things.

Look. Look into their eyes; you're less likely to be distracted when you're looking into their eyes.

Listen. Don't let that voice in your head drown them out. Sometimes to make sure I'm listening, I will repeat in my head what they're saying.

"All you need is love." ~ The Beatles

Life is simple. We just tend to make it complicated. Keep looking for the simple answer. The simplest answer is love. When it comes down to it, being a good parent is based upon love. Loving your children and letting them know that they are loved is the basis of pretty much all parenting. And it is not just loving them; it's also letting them know that they're loved.

When I was in my twenties, I knew a man who had two daughters who were about my age. There's no doubt in my mind that Sam loved those girls with all of *his* heart, but he was absolutely terrible about letting them know that he loved them. They were a traditional family. In other words, they grew up with Mom and Dad, no divorce issues. But they grew up in a home where no one ever expressed their love. No hugging, no saying, "I love you." In essence, no closeness, no affection. Both of those girls are now in their 40's and 50's. They're insecure. Their relationships are mostly failures, and at their core they live in fear.

Their father was a yeller and screamer and he would get angry at the drop of a hat. He was so full of anger and he was bitter about the disappointments he had in his life. From my perspective, his disappointments were no bigger than what everyone else faces, but he always felt picked on. He was the classic victim. None of his failures was ever his fault. He was 100% certain that everything that went wrong in his life was because someone else had treated him badly.

As an outsider, you could see his two girls didn't feel loved; they didn't feel emotionally connected. There was no physical or sexual abuse, and I'm not even sure if his treatment of his girls would qualify as emotional abuse. The worst thing you can say about him is that he spent a lot of time yelling at his wife and at the world in general. He never hugged his kids; he never told them he loved them; he never told them that they looked pretty.

I had been raised in a totally opposite environment. My brothers and I knew, we simply knew, that we were loved, that we were invaluable, that we were important, that people cared about us. The contrast was so powerful that I did something that I never would have imagined. I gave Sam advice. I couldn't help myself even though he had been a parent longer than I had been alive.

One day he was complaining about his disappointment that one of his daughters had done something that was inappropriate and he couldn't figure it out. I just blurted it out: "Why don't you tell them that you love them?" His response was, "I just can't do that; it's not my way; it's not my make-up." I pressed him. I said, "I really think it would help if you would give them a hug once in a while, if you would just simply tell them that you loved them and that they looked nice." I always remember his response. He said, "They know I love them; I'm just not the kind of person that says it."

I'm not judging the man, because I believe he was telling me the truth as he saw it. I believe he was living his life the way he was taught. He couldn't break free from the past. In fact, that was one of his hallmark qualities. He totally lived in the past and constantly re-ran all of the perceived slights and injustices that he believed had been laid at his doorstep.

As we discussed, there are consequences to our actions and there were consequences to his. Is it a coincidence that those two women are both unhappy, fearful, seemingly incapable of forming powerful, emotional connections?

I would amend the Beatles title from "All you need is love" to "All you need is love... and you have to give it."

Following are my rules for Effective Parenting.

Rule #1: Control Your Emotions

The father I described above was an extreme example. He was unable to emotionally connect with his children, let alone to be with them. Unfortunately, his two children grew up to be adults that could not emotionally connect with others. But that rule has so many other parallels.

For example, don't yell at your children. If you yell at children, they do not hear you. Instead, you're simply upsetting them. That doesn't mean if you've yelled at your children, you're going to destroy their psyche. Remember, take the long view. We're building a foundation one brick at a time. None of us is perfect. Yelling at your children and upsetting them once will have no effect on them. Yelling at them the entire time they grow up, well... let's hope that somehow children who have to deal with that eventually learn how to overcome it.

Most of us fall somewhere in the middle. The point here is that it's not effective. It's not promoting your magnificent obsession.

If you're a yeller and a screamer, learn from the example of the old man I just talked about. His excuse was "I can't help it." It's still an excuse and there are still consequences. His children are now damaged adults because their father couldn't control his emotions.

Learn from the mistakes of others.

You Can Do Anything You Want, as Long as You Develop New Habits

It's one thing for me to tell you to control your emotions, or don't yell. It's another thing for you to actually do it. You can do it. Here are two practical steps to help you. First, identify what it is that really triggers that emotion. It's not your children. In my friend's case (the old man above), I suppose it was fear; he was afraid of everything. And for him, the starting point would have been to simply admit to the kids that he was afraid.

It's too late for him and his kids, but it is not too late for you. If you can't control your emotions, figure out what it is that triggers those emotions. For most people, it's some form of fear. Then, begin to form a new way of responding to that fear.

The second step would be to keep in mind your goal of being a great parent and then create a disconnect. Emotions aren't a bad thing. The problem is that we have triggers that release our emotions without thinking. When my daughters were growing up in my home, I gave them a hug and kiss on the cheek or the forehead everyday. I'm not talking about a dainty little hug; I'm talking about a big old bear hug. And I'd give them hugs in front of their friends. Sometimes they'd be embarrassed by it, but as they got older, their friends wanted to hug me.

Even now, with my kids grown up and I don't see them every day, on the days when I do see them, I give them a big old hug and tell them I love them. You may not be the hugging type and although I would encourage you to give it a try, you don't have to be the hugging type. But you've got to let your kids know you love them somehow. There's no exact formula and you have to do what's right for you.

I have a friend who is a single mom and raised two boys by herself. She's not a big hugger – she does hug her kids, but it's not as often or as powerful as I hug mine – but her kids are just as stable. They know they are loved. She does it in her way. She's a great listener and always emotionally available.

Make it a habit to look your children in the eyes every day and listen to them. And let them know in whatever way you find appropriate that you love them.

Rule #2: Be What You Want Them To Be

Even if you've never taken a class in psychology, just about everyone knows that children learn by modeling and the people they model most often are their parents. Everyone says, "I want my children to be happy." Well, are you happy? Do you have honor and integrity? Do you treat people the way you want to be treated? Are you overly materialistic? Are you moody?

This book is not designed to lay any guilt on you. Feeling guilty won't make you a better parent. Too many divorced parents, let alone parents who are not divorced, feel guilty. I personally have friends who grew up in very dysfunctional homes who turned out to be wonderful human beings. You don't have to be perfect. Just be honest with yourself. If there are things you want to change about yourself, then work on it now. Try to be the best human you can be. There's a good chance your children will model your good qualities. Remember, you are a role model.

Rule #3: Love, Not Fear

Most of us make our decisions based on one of two emotions – fear or love. Unfortunately, for most people in this world, they're driven by fear more often than they are by love.

If you want healthy children, teach them to act based on love not fear. Teach them to be in the minority. I can tell you lots of things not to do: Don't be negative, don't be sarcastic, etc. But what we're really talking about is don't cause hurt. Don't belittle anyone and certainly not your children. Don't cause pain. Don't cause fear.

Instead, create love. Build self-confidence. Let your children know they are safe and protected.

I'll give you an example of how not to do it. Remember the sad example above, the old man with the two daughters? One of his daughters relayed a story to me of how when she was in high school she tried on a new dress. She had taken a lot of time to pick this dress out at the mall. She thought it was a beautiful dress and she thought she looked beautiful. She was excited to try it on and show it off for her parents. If you're a parent, you know the look that she had in her eyes. You know how children look when they're excited and looking for approval or praise.

Instead of praise, her dad told her it made her look a little wide in the hips. He was from the old school. He believed children should be humble and not get a big head. She told me that story years after it happened and I could still see the pain in her eyes. He didn't want to hurt her, but he didn't know how to show her love.

Remember how powerful you are in your child's eyes and use that power to create an environment where he or she will make decisions based on love and trust.

One positive way to do that is to build confidence in your children. The starting point for building confidence is to give your children tasks to accomplish, goals to work toward. Children develop confidence from doing. They get stronger when they face their challenges and they ultimately conquer them.

Rule #4: Set Rules And Boundaries

Whatever your rules are, make sure your children understand them and understand the consequences of breaking them. Breaking those rules is bound to happen at some point or another, so be sure you follow through with the consequences – not out of anger or emotion but just because those are the consequences.

Rule #5: Be A Hero

Keep promises. Say what you mean and mean what you say. If you break your promise, then you're a liar. Let your children inspire you to be the best you can be. Children will do as you do, not as you say.

I knew a long time ago I was never going to win the 7th game of the World Series with a home run or win the Super Bowl with a last minute touchdown pass. I also realized when my kids were little that this was my chance to be something more important, a real hero. They didn't ask to be here, but I'm their dad, the only dad they will ever have. My kids deserve a great dad.

I made a commitment a long time ago that I was going to be John Wayne and the Calvary coming to the rescue. No, I don't mean their best friend. I mean their hero, a role model, a guide, the kind of man they would one day look for in a husband, the kind of man they would try to create if they had sons.

I found my meaning in life: I would be great dad. What could be more important than that? No matter what I do with the rest of my life, nothing will be as important as raising my children.

What about you? Will you ever do anything that is more important than raising your children?

Chapter 7 - Things to Consider

❖ Nothing happens "tomorrow".

❖ What is your "magnificent obsession" and are you moving toward it or away from it?

❖ Are you listening?

❖ Are you ruled by love or fear?

Chapter 8

Big Changes, Bigger Opportunities

"If your ship doesn't come in, swim out to it!"
~ Jonathan Winters

Nothing in this book is intended to minimize what you've gone through or what you are going through. And there is nothing here promoting the idea of divorce. This book has been written with the idea that you are already divorced or that it is inevitable.

Embrace Change

People generally don't like change. We resist it, even though we know it's inevitable. Someone once said we're all a little bit insane. That's sort of a dramatic way of getting your attention, but you do have to admit that we all do irrational things. We know that change is inevitable. We know that it will come into our lives, and yet we resist it.

We resist change because we believe it will be painful or we're afraid it's going to be painful. But resisting it is, in itself, painful. So we resist the unknown because it might be painful. To avoid something that might be painful, we create a situation that is painful. That is a little nuts. It all boils down to the fact that we're afraid of the unknown. As discussed in the previous chapter, most of our actions are based on fear or love.

So the other title I thought about giving this chapter was, "Have Courage (You Have No Choice)".

We know change is coming into each and every one of our lives, constantly. And we're good at telling other people not to fear change, but we still fear it. Divorce was certainly a huge change and it caused all kinds of fear of the unknown. But how do we overcome that fear? Let's talk about specific steps you can take to overcome the fear of change.

Have Faith

You could start with a little faith. There really is a higher power. You really are here to learn and to grow.

Maybe that sounds all well and good but it's a little too abstract and New Age for you. So let's talk about the practical side of how all this works and say it as increasing your faith. No doubt, there are many examples in your life of something painful or unknown that you went through that turned out to be a positive thing for you.

If you don't want to look at it from the spiritual point of view, at least we'll look at if from the practical perspective. So the first question I would ask you in this chapter is "Who is important in your life now that you didn't know ten years ago?" If you truly could stop change from happening, you wouldn't know that person because they never would have come into your life.

Take Courageous Risks

I can think of many examples of taking courageous risks in my life. I left a nice safe job with a good salary to start my own business. Most people in my industry are afraid to do that even though they're not that happy in the jobs they have. Leaving a job that's safe and secure causes a certain amount of upset in your life, a certain amount of insecurity. Remember the earlier saying, "On the other side of pain is joy?"

I struck out into the unknown, which meant finding new office space, finding new employees, answering a bunch of questions, literally dealing with the fact that I didn't know what I was doing. The result is that I now have a thriving business working with people I like and I trust. But there's only one way to get there. I had to let go of the past, go through the turmoil of the unknown, and have faith that things would work out.

Maybe one of the things that gave me confidence that it would work out was going through my divorce. Talk about big changes and big opportunities!

I felt as if I was a failure. Everyone in my family had a successful marriage. All of my college roommates had successful marriages. I was the one failure. I would have done almost anything to save my marriage. Lived a lie, or so I thought. My wife concluded that our marriage was over well before I did, so I resisted the change. Talk about pain! Talk about stormy seas! I went from being a young professional in suburbia with the picture-perfect family to being a single dad who had to try to figure out how to raise two girls on his own and keep his business running. At first, I didn't see the opportunity. But what an incredible opportunity it became.

I'm not blaming her. Remember this book is not about blame, but about what an incredible opportunity our divorce became. Because we were two fundamentally different people, we weren't happy together and we could never be happy together. That meant if we had stayed together, our children would have grown up in an unhappy household. There is no doubt in my mind that can be more harmful than growing up in a divorced household. Remember the example of the old man and the two girls in the previous chapter?

So my children did go through trauma and pain, but it passed, and they adjusted to the fact that Mom and Dad had separate houses. And they grew up in a house with me that no longer had strife and tension. What a difference that made! It changed everything for all of us. You don't see that while you're struggling through a divorce, but in hindsight, it was perfectly clear. Because of who we were and how fundamentally different we were from each other, the break up, in the long run, was the best thing for my children.

Create a Stable Environment

The first thing I did after I got a divorce was to set up a stable home for my children. They lived with me, but they spent every other weekend with their mom. I began to date, and for two years I just dated for fun. (That's probably another whole book.) But then, believe it or not, I got tired of dating for fun, and I decided to go out and find a good woman.

I remember very clearly sitting in the bleachers watching one of my daughters cheer for a Peewee football game. My parents had come up for the game and I remember telling my mom that I knew what I wanted.

I wanted to find the girl with the biggest heart. Six months later, I met her. Call it faith, call it coincidence, call it God. But I repeat, you've got to have faith.

Earlier, I mentioned that my ex-wife and I were fundamentally different, that we really couldn't be happy. We were incapable of creating a happy home because we were so different. Now, I had met a woman who was fundamentally similar to me. She had the same values, the same outlook on life. We enjoy each other's company; we enrich one another's life. I would like to think I was a good role model for her two sons and I know, without a doubt, she was a wonderful influence on my two young daughters. We've been together now for over thirteen years. No matter what happens to us, I know that for once in my life, I knew real love. I have a true partner.

Be the Best You Can Be

Stop comparing yourself to others. Stop feeling sorry for yourself. Make a commitment now to simply be the best that you can be. The great thing about that is there is no end to it. You never reach your potential. You just keep getting better and better. You keep evolving to a higher plane.

To really be a great parent and give your children the tools that they'll need to be successful in life, have the strength and courage to always do the right thing where your children are concerned.

Look Back from the End to Move Forward

One last tip: Imagine you're about 85 years-old and your time here is just about done. You're in good health, but you don't have a whole lot of energy left and spend most of your day sitting on the back porch, watching the world. Image it's a beautiful day and you're looking back reviewing your life. What do you see? Do you have regrets? Would you live your life differently? Well, now is your chance. Go out and live it the way you would want to.

One of my favorite movies is *Braveheart*. Most guys know the story; it's a guy movie. If you don't know the story, Mel Gibson is the star playing the title role of William Wallace, a real historical figure who led the Scotsmen against the English when England was the oppressive landlord of Scotland.

The movie takes place several hundred years ago and Mel Gibson's character is the head of all the rebellious Scotsmen whose goal is simple – they want freedom. In the end, the English win and Mel Gibson's character is put to death after having fought many brave battles. Shortly before he is put to death, a woman who loves him is in tears because he is about to die, and he says, "All men die, but few really live." Of course, he really lived as he had lived for a higher purpose (freedom) and he had led men into battle for a noble cause.

Fortunately, you and I don't have to fight people with swords to really live.

But he didn't really live because he chopped someone's head off in battle. He really lived because he served a higher purpose. He served for a noble purpose. He overcame his fear. He really lived because he did what was right, what was necessary in the face of fear.

On the Other Side of Pain is Joy

I share these stories from my life because I hope they'll help you. It's one thing to have faith. It's one thing to say change is good. But I think we learn from concrete examples. I'm sure you have examples like that in your life. And I'm sure there are literally a million people out there who have gone through divorces and successfully raised their children.

You may feel alone and scared, but you're never alone. God is always with you and if you learn to be still, you will hear His voice guiding you. You may not understand why things have turned out the way they have. But they haven't turned out at all. Everything is still evolving. You just can't see the end of the road; none of us can. But believe me, on the other side of pain is joy.

Really Live Your Higher Purpose

You've got a higher purpose, too. Now go out there and really live it.

Chapter 8 - Things to Consider

❖ Change is _____ (fill in the blank).

❖ Who do you know now that you didn't know 10 years ago?

❖ Always keep in mind the 85 year-old on the porch.

A Few Rules to Live By

❖ Be generous. Gratitude is wonderful.

❖ Choose Happiness (Positive Before Negative).

❖ Seek harmony.

❖ Be courageous.

❖ Make sensible decisions. This takes wisdom.

❖ Experience. It is in each of us. It is life.

❖ Seek balance in your life. You will find you smile and laugh more.

❖ Expect the unexpected.

❖ All these points will help you in "Getting Over It!"

Do You Know Someone Who Needs This Book?

Many parents are on a tough road! It is my hope that they can take the wisdom from these pages and make a difference in their lives and the lives of their children. Making this contribution to parents is why I wrote this book. But sometimes the best messages are given to parents from friends and family who care about them.

If you would like to purchase a copy for a parent who "needs to read it" go to any of the following locations:

- www.WisdomForDivorcedParents.com Autographed copies and accompanying gift cards are available. Volume discounts are also available.

- Local bookstores – if it is not on the shelf, they can order it for you!

- Online retailers including Amazon.com, BarnesandNoble.com, Borders.com.

Go to www.WisdomForDivorcedParents.com to order other valuable and helpful products by Len Stauffenger:

- **How To Get Over It: The Workbook**

   Questions for single parents to help you solve some of your own problems, to help you create a Master Plan for raising your kids, and to deal with the pain of your divorce. There's a nurturing coach inside!

- **Getting Over It: Audio CD**

   A delightful listen about the world of single-parenthood from a father's perspective. Warm, witty, and wise advice to help you become the best parent possible.

About the Author

Len Stauffenger, a successful attorney and business owner, is also the divorced father of two daughters, both of whom are now independent, secure, happy young women.

A graduate of Ohio State University (magna cum laude) and the University of Akron Law School (cum laude), Stauffenger served as a former partner with the law firm Stark and Knoll Co., LPA, and the law firm Amer Cunningham Brennan, LPA, prior to establishing his own thriving practice in 2002. He has been named as one of *Cincinnati Magazine*'s "Super Lawyers" for the past six years (2004–2009). In addition, Stauffenger is the owner of Rachel Systems, LLC, a small software company that is involved in creating revolutionary software for use in the field of medical managed care.

A Reiki master who uses his skills to heal and help countless others, Stauffenger is also a self-described "avid student of what makes people tick." In both his professional and his personal endeavors, Stauffenger's driving focus is to help to move forward in life. But, he says, "It is not enough to tell people to move forward.

You have to show them *how* to move forward. You have to teach them how to let go of the past."

Having come through the pain, fear, frustration, and anger of separating from his wife and life partner, Stauffenger has written ***Getting Over It!*** with the authority and empathetic voice of someone who's "been there" – and who found the keys to parenting successfully both during and after divorce.

Stauffenger currently lives in Akron, Ohio.

GETTING OVER IT

Resources

Wisdom For Divorced Parents

Author Len Stauffenger focuses on helping parents move forward in all aspects of life. Len believes that it is not enough to simply tell people to move forward, you have to tell them how to move forward. You have to tell them and teach them how to let go of the past. Len's focus is on how to "get over it" so that you can be successful in all aspects of your life.

Website: www.WisdomForDivorcedParents.com
Contact: Len@WisdomForDivorcedParents.com
MacKenzie Publishing, LLC.
460 White Pond Dr.
Akron, Ohio 44320

Divorced Father's Network

The Divorced Father's Network is a peer-support, non-profit organization dedicated to improving the lives of children, fathers, and mothers, by supporting engaged, effective fathering during and after divorce.

Website: www.divorcedfathers.com
Contact: steve@divorcedfathers.com
(831) 335-5855

Divorced Fathers Network
PO Box 7132
Santa Cruz, CA 95061-7132

Fathers: National Center for Fathering

__Championship Fathering__ is an effort to change the culture for today's children and the children of coming generations. We're seeking to reach, teach, and unleash 6 million dads, creating a national movement that can reverse the negative trends in our society. This movement is characterized by men who will fulfill their commitment to __Love__ their children, __Coach__ their children, __Model__ for their children, __Encourage__ other children, and __Enlist__ other dads to join the team.

Website: www.fathers.com
Contact: http://tinyurl.com/42rnyo
           800-593-DADS or 913-384-4661
           National Center for Fathering
           P.O. Box 413888
           Kansas City, MO 64141

Fatherville

Fatherville is a resource for fathers by fathers and about fathers. We are here to encourage and support dads as they make their journey down the road called fatherhood. Our mission and goal is to encourage men to become better fathers through the exchange of ideas. We believe that when dads communicate and relate their personal tips, tricks, and traps that all fathers can benefit and perhaps avoid some of the pitfalls that will occur on their journey.

Website: www.fatherville.com
Contact: 208-887-9086

Resource Center for Fathers and Families

The mission of the Resource Center for Fathers & Families is to provide resources that will help men become better parents and better parenting partners regardless of marital status, and to provide the model that all children deserve. As a result, communities, families, the family's economy and society in general will benefit.

Website: www.resourcesforfathers.org
Contact: info@resourcesforfathers.org
                  763-783-4938
                  Human Services Building
                  Suite 305
                  1201 89th Avenue NE
                  Blaine, Minnesota 55434

Dads and Daughters

Joe Kelly is a father, author, speaker, activist, editor, and consultant. Author of six books, Joe is a leading voice for progressive parenting, influential advocate for children and families, and a skilled advisor in writing, editing, and publicity for socially responsible organizations.

Website: www.dadsanddaughters.org
Contact: info@dadsanddaughters.org
           (651) 332-0275
           Joe Kelly
           2650 University Ave. West, Suite #101
           Saint Paul, Minnesota 55114

At Home Dad (formerly Slowlane)

Peter Baylies has been a stay-at-home dad for his two sons for 12 years. He writes the At-Home Dad Newsletter, which has been turned into the stay at-home-Dad handbook. Link to his handbook: http://tinyurl.com/ysvdxb

Website:
www.angelfire.com/zine2/athomedad/index.blog
Contact: athomedad@aol.com

Children, Youth and Family Consortium

The Children, Youth, and Family Consortium's website is a bridge to a wide range of information and resources about children and families, connecting research, teaching, policy, and community practice. It seeks to advance greater understanding, shared knowledge, and action.

Website: www.cyfc.umn.edu/welcome.html
Contact: cyfc@umn.edu
           612-625-7849
           MacNamara Alumni Center, Suite 201
           200 Oak Street S. E.
           Minneapolis, MN 55455

Stepfamily Foundation

Beginning in 1976, the Stepfamily Foundation has been guiding the 21st Century Family – the stepfamily – to help it function successfully. No other individual or organization has been devoted full time to the management of this complex family system.

Website: www.stepfamily.com
Contact: Stepfamily@aol.com
           212-877-3244
           Jeannette Lofas Ph.D.

Westbrook University, President
333 West End Avenue
New York, NY 10023

Alliance for Non-custodial Parents Rights

Have issues or questions about your rights in Family Court with regard to child support, custody, or visitation? ANCPR's handbook can help you.

Website: www.ancpr.org
Contact: helpme@ancpr.org

Landmark Education

The Landmark Forum is specifically designed to bring about positive and permanent shifts in the quality of your life. These shifts are the direct cause for a new and unique kind of freedom and power. The freedom to be absolutely at ease no matter where you are, who you're with, or what the circumstance – the power to be in action effectively in those areas that are impor-tant to you.

Website: www.landmarkeducation.com
Contact: Your local Landmark Education office
           415-981-8850

Landmark Education
353 Sacramento St., Ste. 200
San Francisco, CA 94111

The Silva Method

The Silva Method is based on the knowledge that how you think, believe, and behave dictates your living experience. By making simple, positive changes, you can live a powerful life of your own design. The goal of the Silva Method is to teach you how to use more of your brain and activate the untapped areas of your mind.

Website: www.silvamethod.com
Contact: silvamethod@silvamethod.com
          800.545.6463
          Silva International
          P.O. Box 2249
          Laredo, TX 78044-2249